ABOUT TIME

IPPR/Rivers Oram Press

ABOUT TIME

The Revolution in Work and Family Life

Patricia Hewitt

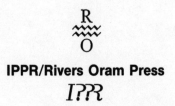

IPPR/Rivers Oram Press

First published in 1993 by
Rivers Oram Press
144 Hemingford Road, London N1 1DE

Published in the USA by
Paul and Company
Post Office Box 422, Concord, MA 01742

Set in 10/12 Sabon by Witwell Ltd, Southport
and printed in Great Britain
by T.J. Press (Padstow) Ltd, Padstow, Cornwall

Designed by Lesley Stewart

British Library Cataloguing in Publication Data
A catalogue record for this book is available from the British Library

ISBN 1-85489-039-5
ISBN 1-85489-040-9 pbk

CONTENTS

TABLES AND FIGURES

Tables

Figures

ACKNOWLEDGEMENTS

Many people have helped me write this book. I want to thank my colleagues at IPPR, particularly Linda Bransbury, Ros Burton, James Cornford, Anna Coote, Judith Edwards, Jane Franklin, Sylvia Hewlett and David Miliband, for discussing ideas, commenting on drafts and offering practical help. Adrienne Burgess, Jack Dromey, Tess Gill, Harriet Harman, Bob Hepple, Paul Ormerod and Gill Sargeant all gave me helpful comments on earlier drafts.

Jay Gershuny, at Nuffield College, Oxford, generously provided material from his time budgets archive; both he and Charles Handy shared with me their enthusiasm for the subject. David Ramsden and Caroline Jones, from B&Q, provided detailed information about their company, as did Gerry Wade and Doug Cornfoot from IBM, and Claire Weaver from TSB. Many trade union officers provided both information and ideas, including Ed Blissett and Doris Hawley of BIFU; Alex Ferry of the Confederation of Shipbuilding and Engineering Unions; John Edmonds and Claire Corker of the GMB; Clive Brook and Jim McAusaon of the IRSF; Jack Dromey and Margaret Prosser of the TGWU; and David Lea and Simon Wilson at the TUC. Bryn Davies at Union Pension Services provided invaluable assistance with the proposal for a 'time bank' scheme. Colette Fagan and David Perfect at the Equal Opportunities Commission supplied additional information from the EOC's Hours of Work Survey.

I am especially grateful to B&Q for their generous grant towards the costs of the qualitative research described in chapter 4, and to Deborah Mattinson and Rachel Nobes of GMA who carried it out. I also want to thank Rupa Huq for her invaluable help in preparing the final text. Needless to say, none of them is responsible for any errors of fact or judgment in what follows.

Finally, my thanks go, as always, to my husband, Bill Birtles, and our children, Alexandra and Nicholas, for whom I wish I had all the time in the world.

Patricia Hewitt
August 1992

INTRODUCTION

For as long as there have been employers and employees, there have been disputes over working hours. As the American union leader, George Meany, said: 'The progress towards a shorter work-day and a shorter work week is a history of the labor movement itself'. After a decade in which weekly working hours actually increased in Britain, the movement for a shorter working week has recently been revived by engineering workers, both here and in West Germany.

In the past, conflict between trades unions and managers about working time usually concerned the hours of full-time workers. The rapid growth in the number of people employed for substantially shorter hours – part-time employees – creates a new dimension to the working time debate. Studies of women's employment have increasingly stressed the need to challenge male patterns of working time and to create a better fit between work and family. As the author of a recent Equal Opportunities Commission study asks: 'should the aim be to make women more like men or men more like women?'[1]

This book brings together these two perspectives – the shorter working hours campaign for full-time, particularly male, employees, and the work/family debate prompted by the experience of female employees – within a wider analysis of how modern systems of production and distribution are changing traditional ways of organising working time. In essence, modern economies are moving from an old model of working time to a new: but public policy has yet to catch up.

Why the old model no longer fits

Public policy in Britain is based on a model of full-time, permanent employment stretching from the completion of full-time education to the onset of full-time retirement and organised around standard working days, weeks and years: '48 hours for 48 weeks for 48 years'. The model can be seen clearly in the social security system, employment law and

1

policies for retirement and pensions. It pervades the culture of business, management and public life. It affects the organisation and strategies of trades unions as well as most discussion of full employment. It indirectly influences decisions in many other policy areas, including transport, leisure provision, child care and the care of elderly dependants. And it profoundly affects and depends upon the organisation of family life.

This model, which was always based on the lives of men rather than women, simply does not fit modern industrial countries. The increase in part-time work, primarily amongst women and particularly in the service sector, is only one source of change. There are several, inter-related factors which are transforming the organisation of working time and working lifetimes.

First, the dramatic increase in employment amongst married women with children. In 1971, nearly two-thirds of the British workforce were men. By 2000, about half will be women. Already, part-time employees form one-quarter of the workforce and that proportion is growing. On present trends, the majority of women in the workforce, and a growing minority of men, can expect to work part-time at some stage in their lives. Part-time employment, parental leave and career breaks all challenge the pattern of continuous, full-time employment.

Second, the increase in other 'non-standard' groups of workers. The growth of part-time employment is not the only relevant change in the workforce. One of the factors explaining the growth in self-employment – one in twelve of the workforce in 1989 and also growing[2] – is the desire for greater control over one's working time. 'Home-workers,' also an expanding group, also work 'in their own time' – although this group includes people with such widely different experience as the mother working late at night for very low wages and the 'telecommuter' enjoying a substantial income as well as substantial freedom. Within the permanent workforce itself, managers have begun to adapt to the religious observances of members of non-Christian religions as well as the needs for special leave of those with families in other parts of the world.

Third, the pressure from men for shorter working hours. Under the banner of '8 hours work, 8 hours rest, 8 hours play', the British trade union movement won reductions in the weekly hours of full-time industrial workers of nearly a third between 1881 and 1981.[3] In the 1980s, the hours of full-time workers in industry increased as overtime expanded, although significant increases were achieved in paid holidays. In the last two years, however, industrial action has succeeded in cutting the basic weekly hours of full-time manual engineering workers from 39 to 37.

Fourth, the shrinking of the working lifetime. At one end, the raising of the school-leaving age; an expansion (although as yet inadequate) in further and higher education; and the rapid rise in youth unemployment during the 1980s have all postponed entry to the labour market. At the other end, the working lifetime has been shortened through earlier retirement – both voluntary, as better-paid employees take advantage of good pension schemes, and involuntary, as older employees are made redundant.

Fifth, the expansion and changing structure of the service sector. Higher disposable incomes and shorter working hours for full-time employees have helped to increase the demand for leisure services. The growth in employment amongst women has increased the demand for services which substitute for domestic labour and for services outside 'normal' hours. The marked drop in Christian worship has changed people's expectations of Sunday activities, one result of which has been a sharp increase in (sometimes illegal) Sunday trading. The increase in the number of very elderly people, combined with the reduction in the number of women available to work as volunteers or to care for relatives full-time, has increased demand for professional domiciliary services during weekends and evenings as well as weekdays.

The '24-hour service economy' may be an exaggeration. But extended opening hours are increasingly common and some enterprises – not only the emergency services – do operate round the clock and round the year. Employers seeking to extend their operating hours to meet changing demand as well as to hold down labour costs and prices, increasingly turn to part-time and other forms of 'flexible' employment.

Sixth, the pressure within manufacturing industry for longer and more flexible operating hours. Expensive, high-tech equipment cannot generally be left idle for long periods if it is to justify its capital costs. Competitive pressures (which will intensify further with the development of the European Single Market) require a reduction in unit costs. For many enterprises, both factors point to an extension of operating hours. The increased need for labour may be met by increased overtime. But a new strategy is emerging in response to the combination of competitive pressures, employee demands for shorter working hours, the costs of overtime and (particularly in the South-East) the difficulty of recruiting skilled full-time workers: decoupling factory operating hours from individual working hours. The result is shorter and more flexible working time arrangements within the manufacturing as well as the service sector.

Seventh, the post-war transformation in international communications. Any business operating internationally has seen its working hours extended by telephone, fax and computer communications across different time-zones. Within the financial sector, for!instance, dealings on the Stock Exchange open and close five hours later in New York, and nine hours earlier in Tokyo and Sydney than in London. But any enterprise which trades or operates internationally operates on more than one clock. Even within Europe, there is a two-hour time difference between some members of the European Community and three hours or more between Britain and Russia. And computer operations (albeit with little staffing) may take place round-the-clock and round-the-world, as an enterprise in one country takes advantage of cheap-time computing facilities in another continent.

Eighth, the need for education, training and retraining throughout – and not simply as a preparation for – the working lifetime. The central factor of success in modern industrial economies is the level of human, rather than financial, capital. No longer can qualifications acquired before the age of 20 see an individual through a working life. Educational and training leave is still rare in Britain; in the future, it will need to become part of the normal working lifetime.[4]

Women's work, men's work

The old model of full-time, life-time employment was a male model. It never fitted the discontinuous employment patterns of the majority of women. Nor did it encompass women's unpaid work in the home. Working time is structured in radically different ways for women and for men. Put at its simplest, the time men spend in paid employment determines how much time they have for their families: the time women spend caring for their families determines how much time they have for paid employment. As a result, the pattern of women's working lifetimes, as well as the organisation of their working time over the week and the year, are very different from those of men.

As more women remain in or rejoin the labour force after having children, the tensions between 'work' and 'family' become more acute. The assumption that men will earn and women will care was never true for working-class families. Today, the most common household type is two adults who are both earners and parents.[5] But the division of paid and unpaid labour was also a division of paid and unpaid time. While women have moved into the workforce and substantially increased their paid labour time, men have not moved back into the home or increased the time they spend in unpaid domestic work at the same rate. This unequal division of labour – women's 'double burden' – underlies persistent inequalities between women and men in the workplace. If we are to resolve the conflict between family and work, and to equalise opportunities in the workplace, then we will have to redistribute time between men and women as well as between the workplace and the home.

Industrial and 'post-industrial' time

In agricultural communities, the seasons of the year and the passage of the sun govern the rhythm of working life. Industrialisation involves the growing regulation by employers of their employees' time. E. P. Thompson concludes that 'Mature industrial societies of all varieties are marked by time-thrift and by a clear demarcation between "work" and "life".'[6] Developing this theme, two American labour historians argue that '[In agricultural communities] the unit of labor was the task, not the hours, and a good working day was measured by the portion of field ploughed or the number of rows harvested. . . . Only later, with the expansion of markets and with increased demand for goods by merchant capitalists, did the employer conceive of work less in terms of tasks than of time spent in the orderly pursuit of routinized production.'[7]

With industrialisation came contracts regulated by hours worked, rather than task performed. As Thompson puts it: 'Time is now currency: it is not passed but spent'. 'Time is money' means time and motion studies, time management, clocking on and off, saving time, filling Kipling's 'unforgiving minute'. In many industrial towns in Britain, the rhythm of the year as well as the day and week was set by major employers, with the entire community – schools as well as factories and most shops – closing for one or two weeks during the summer. 'Fordist' production techniques – mass production of mass consumption goods – also meant a 'fordist' organisation of time.

There were, of course, substantial variations in what 'full-time' meant to different groups: for manual workers in factories, shiftwork, night-work, clocking on and overtime; in offices and much of retailing, '9 to 5'; in schools, 8.30 a.m. to 3.30 p.m. with the year punctuated by half-terms and seasonal holidays, and so on. But there was a general expectation, corresponding to the general organisation of work, that people performing the same task within the same organisation or sector would do so within the same times – and that those times would be set by the employer.

That is changing. Flexitime, four-day weeks or nine-day fortnights, weekend-only jobs, term-time working, new shift arrangements which combine shorter individual working hours with longer operating hours, 'week on, week off' contracts, annual hours contracts, voluntary shorter hours working, a wide variety of part-time arrangements, individual choice of working hours and so on: all undermine the standard form of full-time employment. Not every enterprise is moving in the same way, and there are still many organisations where most or all employees work standard full-time hours. But only a minority of employees now work a 'normal working day', and the 'normal working week' is becoming a minority activity too. The pressure for more flexible working hours is insistent, not only in Britain but throughout the European Community and other industrialised countries.

From the old model to a new

The disappearance of the full-time, life-time housewife and mother; the growing demands of 'household production' and self-servicing; the changes in conditions of production which I noted earlier; and the crowding of leisure time which follows from rising productivity and rising real incomes: all these suggest that the pressure on working time is unlikely to be reversed.

The organisation of working time is becoming more flexible, more varied and more individualised. We can see emerging from the old model of standardised working time a new model of 'post-industrial' working time – a model much closer to female, than to male, patterns of the past.[8]

There is amongst many feminists and trade unionists a suspicion that 'flexibility' in working time, as well as other aspects of employment, is only a disguise for cutting real wages and intensifying work. There are undoubtedly employers who have used it in just that way. But underlying at least some of the suspicion of flexibility is an unstated assumption that 'real' employment is full-time, life-time employment, with anything else inevitably a second-best alternative. This book challenges that assumption and the model to which it belongs, and suggests a different approach to working time.

In the first half, I consider the detailed evidence of changes in working time. Chapter 1 deals with the changes in the working hours and lifetime working patterns of women and men. Chapter 2 presents detailed examples of new working time arrangements in Britain and other European countries. Chapter 3 deals with time spent on unpaid work in the home and chapter 4 analyses public attitudes towards working time questions, drawing both on published surveys and on qualitative research commissioned by IPPR for this report.

The second half deals with policy implications. Chapter 5 considers the objectives of working time reform and the possible conflicts between them. Chapter 6 deals with national and European regulation of working time. Chapters 7 and 8 look at what managers and unions need to do at the workplace to make flexibility work, as far as possible, for all concerned.

IPPR has already published two reports from its working time project: *The Time of Our Life*, dealing with flexible retirement and other issues affecting older workers; and *Working Time: A New Legal Framework*, analyzing developments in employment law and the proposed new European Community Directives. In a future book, *Escaping from Dependency*,[9] we will be proposing detailed reforms of social security and taxation which, together with new labour market strategies, will enable those now trapped in poverty to combine paid employment and parenthood.

1 WORKING LIFETIMES AND WORKING HOURS

Everybody knows that industrialised societies today work shorter hours and enjoy more leisure. Or do we?

Compared with the last century, or even with several decades ago, working hours have indeed fallen. But the picture is far more complicated than that. The reduction in full-time employees' hours was halted and reversed during the 1980s: men in Britain now work longer hours on average than in any other European Community country. For women, the most dramatic change has not been a drop in working hours, but an *increase* in the paid working lifetime.

Partly because of the growth in part-time employment, the normal working day and the normal working week – 9 to 5, Monday to Friday – can no longer be taken for granted. The 'normal' working day is already a minority activity; the 'normal' working week rapidly becoming so. Even our notion of the normal working lifetime is being challenged by later entry to the workforce, earlier and more flexible retirement and, in between, breaks occasioned by the demands of family.

I start by looking at how men and women's working lifetimes are changing, before turning to the length and organisation of the working week and the working year.

Men's working lifetimes

In the century before 1981, as Table 1.1 shows, the hours worked by men over their lifetimes fell by 43%. By the early 1980s, lifetime hours were little over half those of the 1880s.

More impressionistically, Charles Handy has suggested that 'the lifetime job' is falling from 100,000 hours for his generation to 50,000 for his children's. The 100,000 was made up of 47 hours for 47 weeks of 47 years; the 50,000 could be 37 hours for 37 weeks of 37 years (shorter hours, longer holidays, more education and earlier retirement) or 45 hours for 45 weeks for 25 years (a demanding 'core job' ending at around the

Table 1.1: Annual and lifetime hours of work (men) Great Britain

	1881	**1981**	**% fall**
Hours per week	59.0	41.7	29 %
Weeks per year	50.5	45.9	9 %
Hours per year	2,980	1,914	36 %
Years in labour force	56	48	14 %
Lifetime hours	154,000	88,000	43 %

Source: B. Williams, OECD Social Affairs, Manpower and Education Directorate (February 1984); and 'Shorter Hours - increased employment' *Three Banks Review*, September 1984.

age of 50) or 25 hours for 45 weeks of 45 years (continuous part-time work).[1] It should be noted, however, that Handy's '100,000 hours' was a *male* lifetime job, and not that of most women with children.

Despite the substantial drop in total hours which has taken place, the *shape* of men's working lives has not yet fundamentally altered. Men's lives are still a sandwich: education and retirement, with full-time employment in between. The large-scale National Training Survey in the mid-1970s, for instance, confirmed the male pattern of 'continual attachment' to the workforce: three-quarters of male respondents had worked continuously since leaving school.[2] By comparison, most women's initial entry to full-time employment after education is interrupted at the birth of their first child.

Later in, earlier out

What has changed, however, is the age at which both men and women enter and leave the workforce. A higher school-leaving age and expansion of education and training after school have begun to postpone employment for young people. Widespread concern about the low proportion of 16 to 18 year-olds remaining in full-time education in Britain compared with other industrial countries has led to proposals for a statutory requirement that young employees be released for a day or more education each week, with the eventual aim of retaining most of this age-group in full-time education.

In the 1970s and 1980s, furthermore, very high unemployment amongst young people meant an even lengthier postponement of entry to full employment. The Women and Employment Survey traced the lifetime employment patterns of over 5,000 women aged between 16 and 59 in 1980. In 1939, when the oldest women in the survey were aged between 15 and 19, nine out of ten were in employment – a proportion that remained unchanged amongst each successive cohort until the late 1960s. (Full-time students of this age were excluded from the analysis.) By 1974, the proportion in employment amongst non-students aged between 16 and 19 had dropped to 85% and, by 1979, to eight out of ten.[3]

At the other end of the working lifetime, the age of leaving full-time employment has also been substantially reduced by the fall in official and unofficial retirement ages. In recent decades, extensive redundancies in industry effectively retired many men in their 50s. Many men in their early 60s are forced by ill-health or disability into early retirement, while the spread of occupational pension schemes has made early retirement an attractive option for others.

A decade less in employment

Thus, pressures at both ends have substantially reduced the length of men's working lifetimes. Men born between 1900 and 1910 who lived to reach their 60s in the 1960s had an average working lifetime of 51 years (including, of course, one or both world wars) between leaving school at 14 and reaching the age of 65. Even after that age, one-quarter of this generation was still in employment, extending the average working lifetime even further.

For men born in the 1920s, reaching their 60s in the 1980s, the working lifetime had already dropped to around 48 years. Barely half of men aged 60–64 were still in employment by the late 1980s and the proportion remaining in work after the age of 65 fell to below 8%.[4] The Organisation for Economic Co-operation and Development (OECD) reports a sharp decline in employment for men aged over 55 in almost all industrial countries, from between one-third and one-half 20 years ago to between one-fifth and one-third today.[5]

If the trend towards earlier retirement continues, the male working lifetime will drop to around 40 years (from 18 to 58); an extension of education and training would reduce that figure even further. Men born near the end of this century can expect a working lifetime at least a decade shorter than those born in the early 1900s.

Nonetheless, even after a decade of very high unemployment, and despite later entry and earlier retirement, most men can still expect a straightforward progress from full-time education through full-time employment to full-time retirement. For women who never have children, the picture is similar, although for a minority of older women, the need to care for an ageing relative forces a move to part-time employment or out of employment altogether.

Women's working lives

For the majority of women – those who have children – the picture is very different. First, whereas the typical male pattern is of continuous employment, the typical female pattern is of discontinuous employment, with one or more breaks from paid work caused by domestic responsibilities.

Second, although the great majority of men actually follow the typical male pattern of education/work/retirement, the 'typical' female pattern is in fact made up of a wide variety of *different* employment histories.

The 1975–76 National Training Survey demonstrates both differences. Three-quarters of the men surveyed had worked continuously since leaving school, with an average of 23 years in employment. The women, however, fell into five different groups. One in five had been continuously employed since leaving education, but for an average period of less than half the men's: in addition to women without children, they included the younger women who had not yet had children. Another, slightly larger group, were out of the labour force at the time of the survey, having spent an average of 8 years in employment followed by an average of 11 years with family responsibilities. A further group, around one quarter, had returned to employment after one break for family responsibilities (their initial period of employment also averaged 8 years, followed by an average of 9½ years at home before their return to paid work). Two smaller groups, each about one in ten, had each had two breaks in their employment history.[6]

Similarly, the Women and Employment Survey revealed *several* 'typical' female working patterns: the 'domestic career' with a lengthy and uninterrupted period at home after the first child is born; the 'phased' work history, with periods of part-time work between and after the birth of children; and the 'continuous career' interrupted, if at all, only by brief periods of maternity leave.[7] Furthermore, working patterns vary with ethnic origin, with Afro-Caribbean women more likely and Asian women less likely to be working full-time. These different patterns need to be kept in mind when looking at aggregate figures.

The third difference between women's and men's working lives lies in the changing amount of time spent in paid employment. While men's working lifetime is becoming steadily shorter, the *paid* working lifetime

11

of women with children is becoming steadily longer. Over the last 30 years, as men and childless women have enjoyed a shift from work to leisure, women with children have experienced a move from family work to paid work.

More employment, less family

A number of factors account for this change. First, the proportion of women in employment has been increasing for every age-group except the youngest. The largest increases were amongst women in their 30s, with employment rates in this age-group increasing by 50% between the 1950s and 1979.

It is now very rare for women never to return to employment after having children: the Women and Employment survey found that amongst women whose children were grown up, one in eight of those whose first child was born in the early 1940s had never returned to work compared with only one in twenty of those with a first child born twenty years later.[8]

Second, the period of time which women spend out of the labour force after having children has been falling dramatically. Amongst women whose first child was born in the early 1950s (the 'Bowlby' years, when it was widely believed that almost any separation from the mother would damage the child), it was five years before a quarter of them had returned to work and nearly ten years before half had done so. Amongst women whose first child was born between 1975 and 1979, a quarter returned to work within *one* year and over half had done so within five years.

Since most women in both periods will have more than one child, the period at home after the *first* child's birth may only be part of the total period at home with children. For those who completed their family in the early 1950s, the median period out of employment (i.e. the point at which half had returned to work) for women returning to work after the birth of the *last* child was eight years. For women having their 'latest' child in the late 1970s (including some whose families were not in fact complete by the time of the survey), the median period out of work after this birth had dropped to 3½ years.

A more recent survey by the Policy Studies Institute confirms that the period out of employment is continuing to fall. Amongst women who had been in work before having a baby in 1988, one half were back at work within nine months, and another fifth were looking for work. A comparable survey in 1979 had found (like the Women in Employment

Survey) that only one-quarter of women returned to work within nine months of giving birth.[9]

Thus, in the 1950s it was eight years before half the women with children returned to work. In the 1970s, it was less than four years. In the 1980s, it was less than one year.[10] In the space of only four decades, the typical experience of motherhood has changed from leaving the workforce for an extended period, to a few years' career break, to maternity leave of less than twelve months.

Third, it is increasingly common for women to return to work *between* having children. According to the Women and Employment survey, only a quarter of mothers whose last child was born in the late 1950s returned to work between births, compared with nearly half of those whose latest child was born in the late 1970s. The PSI study found that about one-third of women expecting their second or third baby, and over one-fifth of those expecting their fourth, were in employment when they became pregnant – in all cases, an increase since the equivalent survey in 1979.

A decade more in employment

On the basis of the Women and Employment Survey, Jean Martin and Ceridwen Roberts estimated the proportion of women's working lifetimes spent in paid employment (for women without as well as those with children). The oldest women, those born between 1920 and 1924, had spent over half of the years between leaving school and the age of 60 in paid employment; by comparison, those born between 1956 and 1960 could expect to spend two-thirds of their working lives in paid employment. For the oldest group, paid employment occupied about 26 years in a total working lifetime of 45 years (15 to 60): for the youngest, paid employment is expected to take nearly 28 years in a working lifetime three years shorter (18 to 60).[11]

But these figures are based on the cautious assumption that 1980 employment rates will remain unchanged. Even if high unemployment persists amongst younger people, it is already clear that employment rates for women with children are continuing to rise, that the period out of employment after childbirth is continuing to decline and that employment between births will continue to increase. The Department of Employment forecasts that a further 500,000 women will join the labour force between 1991 and 2000, making women 44% of the total labour force.[12] The Henley Centre for Forecasting, however, predicts that women will form a majority of British workers.[13]

Some of today's younger women may interrupt or end their employment in order to care for an elderly relative or to retire at the same time as a husband who is older or himself taking early retirement. Nonetheless, it is reasonable to conclude that the Women and Employment Survey predictions under-state the years of paid work and over-state the years of home responsibilities for women who have recently started employment.

Thus, out of a working lifetime of 42 years (18 to 60), a 'typical' pattern in future might include a total of no more than three years at home full-time with children, a further two years for other domestic responsibilities and two years out of the labour market for non-domestic reasons, leaving 35 years in paid employment. Unlike men, today's young women can expect to add a decade of paid employment to their working lifetimes, compared with women born early in this century.

Less full-time, more part-time

So far, I have simply looked at the years women spend in and out of paid employment without distinguishing between full-time and part-time work. But one of the most dramatic changes in the last three decades has, of course, been the increase in part-time employment amongst women in every age-group.

Definitions of 'part-time' vary considerably; I use the term to refer to those working up to 30 hours a week. Between 1951 and 1981, the number of part-time employees rose by over 4 million. As Table 1.2 shows, by September 1991, there were 5.6 million part-time employees (men and women) in Great Britain and a further 0.5 million part-time self-employed workers. Part-time workers, most of them women with children, make up one-quarter of the workforce.[14]

Between 1954 and 1974, the proportion of women aged between 25 and 34 who were working part-time more than doubled, to around one in four;[15] by 1989, it had risen again, to four in ten. A majority of women in every age-group over 35 now work part-time.[16]

Even if only one-quarter of the workforce works part-time at any one time, however, a larger proportion work part-time at some stage in their lives. Many of the younger women without children who are now working full-time can be expected to have children in the future and to work part-time for at least some years after doing so.

Part-time work is also attractive to those nearing retirement age, or those seeking a gradual transition from full-time employment to full-time retirement; in response to demographic pressures, some employers, particularly in the south-east, are already retaining or recruiting older

Table 1.2 Part-time working in Britain, 1991

	Men	Women	Total
		(millions)	
Employees	11.2	10.3	21.5
Part-time	1.0	4.6	5.6
Part-time as %	9%	45%	26%
Self-employed	2.3	.7	3.0
Part-time	.2	.3	.5
Part-time as %	9%	43%	17%
Total workforce	13.5	11.0	24.5
Part-time	1.2	4.9	6.1
Part-time as %	9%	45%	25%

Source: Employment Department Group

workers as part-timers. (See below, p.80, for a discussion of older workers' attitudes to part-time work.)

Until recently, the increased employment amongst mothers of young children today was almost entirely accounted for by the increase in part-time working. Amongst women whose first child was born in the late 1940s, only 5% returned to work *full-time* within six months of the birth, a proportion which was little higher (at 8%) in the late 1970s. Although the overall proportion of first-time mothers returning to work within six months nearly doubled between the late 1940s and the late 1970s, to about one in six, the increase was mainly accounted for by the increase in *part-time* working.[17]

By the late 1980s, however, a woman who had been working full-time when she became pregnant was just as likely to return to full-time as to part-time work. Since 1979, according to the PSI surveys, the proportion of women returning to work within nine months of the child's birth had increased from 25% to 45%. But even more strikingly, the proportion of mothers working *full-time* within that period had increased much faster than the proportion working part-time.[18]

The changes in women's paid working time, therefore, present a far more complicated picture than those for men. Women were less likely to be employed forty years ago, but those who were employed worked longer hours. Today, women are more likely to be in employment and to spend more of their lives in employment: but the hours they work are considerably shorter, both because of the drop in full-time hours and the dramatic increase in part-time employment.

Superficially, women's working lives appear to be converging with those of men, as time spent in family responsibilities is reduced. But the impact of families on paid employment and the extent of part-time working amongst women actually create very different patterns.

Changes in weekly and annual working hours

The campaign for shorter working hours has been central to the trade union movement since its creation in the last century. Basic working hours have declined significantly, from around 47 hours for full-time male manual workers in the 1920s and 1930s, to around 44 hours in the 1940s, 1950s and early 1960s, to 40 hours in the late 1960s, 1970s and 1980s – and moving to 39 hours and below by the early 1990s.

Actual working hours, however, have generally been longer. In 1951, for instance, manual working men worked an average, actual working week of 48 hours. By 1971, that had fallen to 44.7 hours and by 1981, to 43½ hours. During the 1980s, however, the hours actually worked by full-time male manual workers *increased*, largely because of overtime working, to 44.7 hours in 1987 and over 45 hours in 1988, 1989 and 1990. In other words, the average male manual worker's hours were as high in 1987 as they had been in 1971, and higher at the end of the 1980s than they had been twenty years earlier. By 1991, as the recession deepened, average male manual hours were down again, to 43.7.[19]

Figure 1.1 illustrates the changes in all manual workers' hours between 1943 and 1985.

Hours worked by full-timers vary substantially between manual and non-manual workers and between occupational and industrial sectors. For instance, according to the New Earnings Survey, six out of ten men in white-collar jobs have a *basic* week of 38 hours or below, while six out of ten men in manual jobs have a basic week of 38 hours or more. One in five security guards have a basic week of over 44 hours, as do one in ten of those working in catering.[20]

British men: the longest hours in Europe

The recent Hours of Work Survey for the Equal Opportunities Commission found even longer working hours, both contractual and actual, than the New Earnings Survey (NES). (One reason for the difference may be that the EOC survey relied on direct interviews with individuals, rather than employers' returns.) Whereas the NES found that only one in twenty

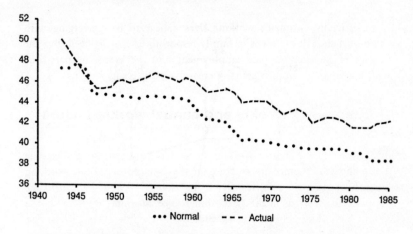

(*Source*: R. Price and G. S. Bain, 'The Labour force', in A. H. Halsey (ed.), *British Social Trends Since 1990*, Macmillan 1988)

Figure 1.1 Normal and actual hours of work of manual workers, 1943–85

men and one in a hundred women full-time employees had *contractual* weekly working hours of over 40, one in three men and one in five women in the EOC survey reported basic hours above this level.[21]

The EOC found that *actual* working hours in the survey week were even higher. As Figure 1.2 illustrates, half of men worked over 44 hours a week; one quarter worked over 50 hours a week, including one in ten who worked over 60 hours a week. Long working hours were particularly prevalent amongst male managers (with a median working week of 52 hours), manual operatives (50-hour week), manual workers in sales (49-hour week) and men doing white-collar professional and technical jobs (47-hour week).

British men work longer hours than men in almost any other European Community country. Within the EC as a whole, two men in ten work an average 46 hours or more a week: in Britain, four in ten do so.[22]

Even within manufacturing industry, where the hours worked by men are often extremely long, there have been some dramatic reductions in working time achieved through a reorganisation of shift patterns and, in many cases, through industrial action. The engineering workers' campaign, described in the next chapter, has won real cuts in working hours.

The working hours of full-time women employees are significantly

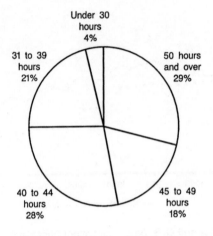

(*Source*:1989 Labour Force Survey)

Figure 1.2 British men's weekly working hours

shorter than those of men (see Figure 1.3). For instance, in 1988, one-third of all full-time male employees worked over 42 hours a week, compared with about one in twelve full-time women employees. Two-thirds of women full-timers worked below 38 hours a week, compared with only one-third of men.[23] In 1991, according to the Department of Employment, women worked on average nearly four hours less than men in full-time manual jobs, and two hours less in full-time non-manual jobs. The EOC survey again reported higher working hours than the Department of Employment, but with women's hours still lower than those of men. For instance, median weekly working hours of full-time women employees were 41, compared with 44 for men. And one in ten of these women full-time employees reported actually working below 28 hours in the survey week.

When domestic work is taken into account, however, the difference between men's and women's working hours largely disappears. Women who are responsible full-time for the care of children have working hours at least as long as those of men in the most demanding jobs (see below).

The self-employed

Amongst the growing number of self-employed, we find again that women generally work shorter hours than men.[24] Nearly six out of ten

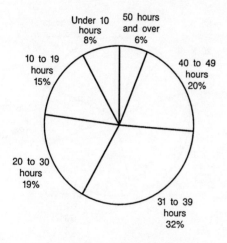

(*Source:*1989 Labour Force Survey)

Figure 1.3 British women's weekly working hours

self-employed men aged between 25 and 60 work over 41 hours a week, and about a quarter work over 57 hours a week. By contrast, half of self-employed women in the same age-group work below 33 hours a week. Reflecting patterns amongst employees, dependent children reduce self-employed women's average working hours but increase men's. For instance, one-third of self-employed fathers of children under the age of ten worked over 57 hours a week, compared with only one in ten self-employed mothers. One-third of the mothers worked between 12 and 32 hours a week, compared with only 4% of the self-employed fathers.

Self-employment increases substantially with age. In 1991, when about one in eight of the total workforce were self-employed, nearly one-third of those working over the age of 65 were. But the hours worked by older self-employed people are considerably lower than average. One in three self-employed men aged 65 and over, and an even higher proportion of women aged 60 and over work 12 hours a week or less, compared with less than one in twenty of those aged between 60 and 65.

Holidays

While weekly working hours were rising during the 1980s, the length of paid annual holidays was also increasing. In 1980, just over half of manual full-time employees had at least five weeks' holidays in addition

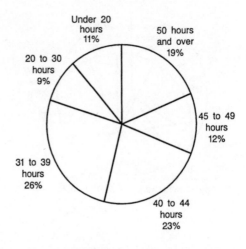

(*Source*:1989 Labour Force Survey)

Figure 1.4   Weekly working hours, British men and women

to public and customary holidays. By 1986, that proportion had increased to nearly nine in ten.[25] The rest had between four and five weeks' holidays. In 1980, one-quarter of manual employees had basic holidays of four weeks or below; by 1986, however, the Department of Employment recorded *no* manual employees falling into this category.

A full-time male manual worker, therefore, during the 1980s saw an hour's increase in his average working week combined with a week's reduction in his average working year. Hours of work have not been reduced (indeed, the average working year has increased slightly), but there has been a shift in the direction of longer blocks of leisure time. It remains to be seen whether the trade unions' success in winning a shorter basic working week will be translated into shorter hours actually worked.

The hours worked by part-timers

The hours worked by part-timers vary considerably. The 1980 Women and Employment Survey found that the hours of part-timers averaged 18½ a week, with part-time employees in nursing working an average of 22 hours and part-time teachers an average of 13 hours a week. The EOC survey found that the median working week for women part-time employees was 17½ hours. One in ten worked over 30 hours and the same proportion below five hours a week.

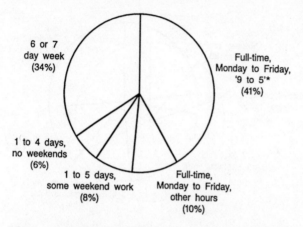

(*Source*: Calculated from Marsh, *Hours of Work EOC*, 1991)
* '9 to 5' means those starting work between 8 am and 10 am,
and finishing between 4 pm and 6 pm

Figure 1.5   The 'normal' working week: British men

In contrast with the recent increase in full-time hours, the hours worked by part-time employees have been falling. Between 1979 and 1990, the proportion of women in part-time manual jobs working below 16 hours a week increased from three in ten to over four in ten. Amongst non-manual part-time women workers, the proportion rose from 23% to 32%.[26] The number of jobs offering below 16 hours a week has grown even faster than those offering higher part-time hours. Sixteen hours is, of course, a vital dividing-line in employment protection law.

Non-standard working hours

Much of the debate about working time flexibility has focused on non-standard working hours – evening, night-time, weekend and shift work. According to several surveys, a surprisingly high proportion of the workforce already works such hours.

Weekends

The 1980 Women and Employment Survey found that one in eight full-time women workers and one in twelve part-time women workers had worked for six or seven days in the previous week. (The report does not

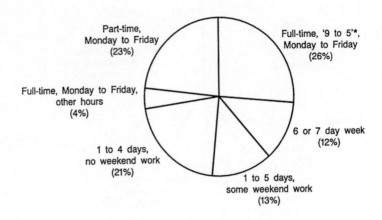

(*Source*: Calculated from Marsh, *Hours of Work EOC*, 1991)
* '9 to 5' means those starting work between 8 am and 10 am,
and finishing between 4 pm and 6 pm

Figure 1.6 The 'normal' working week: British women

separate out those part-timers working weekends whose working week was five days or less.)

A detailed survey of working time preferences carried out for the Jim Conway Foundation in 1988 found that one-third of respondents worked most or every weekend. Only one-third of full-time employees, compared with two-thirds of part-timers, never worked weekends. One in six part-timers, compared with one in eight full-timers, worked *every* weekend, although full-timers were much more likely than part-timers to work 'most' weekends. Nearly another one-third of those surveyed worked occasional weekends.[27]

More recently, the EOC survey found that nearly half the sample had worked on a Saturday in the previous month. This included over half of the men, over one-third of women full-time and one-third of women part-time employees. Over one-third of men, one-quarter of women full-timers and nearly one-fifth of women part-timers had also worked on a Sunday.

Shift work

A survey of employers by ACAS in 1987 found that shiftworking was the most common form of flexibility in hours of work. Over one-quarter of respondents had introduced shiftworking in the last three years, with

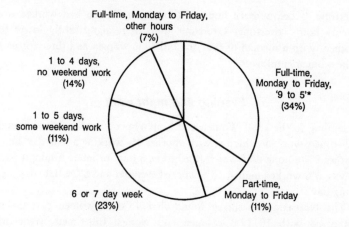

(*Source*: Calculated from Marsh, *Hours of Work EOC*, 1991)
* '9 to 5' means those starting work between 8 am and 10 am,
and finishing between 4 pm and 6 pm

Figure 1.7   The 'normal' working week: British men and women

another one-fifth planning to introduce it or increase its scope. Not surprisingly, shiftwork was most common in the manufacturing, mining and chemicals industries, and in the food and drink sector, with almost no use of shiftworking in banking or public administration.[28]

Overtime

The Jim Conway Foundation survey found that half its respondents had at least some opportunity to work overtime. Amongst those offered overtime work, over half the full-timers and one-third of the part-timers had overtime opportunities most weeks or every week. But most overtime workers averaged less than five hours' overtime a week.

A survey in Northampton found over half of male full-timers, over one-quarter of female full-timers and one in six female part-timers working 'frequent overtime'. Overtime was much less common for women with children aged under five, and less common for those with children aged between five and sixteen, than for those without children. Amongst men, however, overtime was rather more common for those with dependent children than for those without.[29]

The EOC survey found that one-quarter of the men, one-fifth of women full-time and about one in seven women part-time employees had worked overtime in the survey week. Half of the men had worked overtime of below seven hours, although one in ten had worked over twenty hours' overtime. Overtime hours were significantly lower for women, with a median of four for full-time women and three for part-time women employees.

Evening and night work

According to the 1980 Women and Employment Survey, 2% of women full-timers worked at nights, with another 4% working a 'late day' and a further 8% a 'long day' which finished at 6 p.m. or later. Amongst part-timers, 3% worked nights, 13% worked evenings and 8% a 'late day' or a 'long day'.

The Northampton survey found that 15% of women part-timers, compared with 10–12% of men and women full-timers, frequently worked at night. Amongst this sample, frequent night work was most common for women with children under five, suggesting that some mothers were taking part-time jobs at a time when their partners could be home to care for the children.

Amongst the EOC survey respondents, over half the men had worked after 6 p.m. on at least one occasion in the previous month, including one in four who had worked after 11 p.m. and one in seven who had worked overnight. Amongst women full-time employees, nearly half had worked after 6 p.m., including one in eight after 11 p.m. and one in twenty overnight. And amongst women part-time employees, one-third had worked after 6 p.m., including one in ten after 11 p.m., and one in twenty-five overnight. Thus, about one in four men and one in ten women at least occasionally work after 11 p.m.

As the EOC report notes: 'there were women to be found doing what might be considered to be every kind of unsocial pattern of work . . . it suggests that there is no absolute practical or social prohibition on women doing these forms of work [although] that does not mean that they all want to do it, or would be happy about taking on a job which involved it.'[30]

Leisure

Despite the longer hours worked by men in full-time jobs, they enjoy more leisure time than women in full-time employment. On average, a full-time male worker gets 48 hours a week leisure, compared with only 31 hours for a woman in a full-time job. The difference is, of course, the result of women doing more domestic work (the subject of chapter 3). The full-time housewife (a group which includes some women without children) enjoys more leisure than full-time employees, with retired people, as one would expect, enjoying the longest leisure – 92 hours a week for retired men and about 75 hours for retired women.[31]

Jay Gershuny's analysis of time budgets (described in more detail below, see p.51) suggests that, for the population as a whole, leisure time increased by about half an hour a day – 3½ hours a week – between the early 1960s and mid-1980s. By 1985, the average British man was enjoying 37 hours' leisure a week, the average woman about an hour less.

A new map of working time

The full-time employee working a standard, five-day week is in the minority. Figures 1.2 – 1.7 illustrate the new map of working time. As they suggest, the British workforce is segmented not only by sex and by occupational status, but also by working time arrangements. Policy-makers can no longer assume that most people fit within a single, working time norm.

2 NEW WAYS OF WORKING

The picture of working time presented so far is unlikely to remain settled. The influences referred to earlier – changes in the composition of the workforce; the growing demand for services at evenings and weekends; the impact of information technology and competitive pressures on industry; and the campaign by employees and their trades unions for reduced and re-organised working hours – will all continue to undermine the standard working day, week and year.

In considering how working time will change in future, and what kinds of changes we would prefer, we need to look at the innovations which have already been made in working time organisation, both in Britain and elsewhere. Although many of these only affect a minority of workers, they suggest the direction in which more employers are likely to move in future.

Inevitably, different working patterns overlap. Part-time employment, job-sharing and individualised working hours may end up looking like the same thing. In this chapter, I use the generally accepted categories in order to guide the reader through a wealth of case-studies. But part of my aim in building up this detailed picture of the changes taking place is to suggest that the categories we now use for thinking about working arrangements are out of date.

Flexitime

The introduction of flexitime was the main working time change of the 1970s. Because it provided benefits to employees with little cost – indeed real benefit – to employers, it rarely gave rise to industrial conflict.

The ACAS survey in 1987 defined flexible working hours as 'any arrangement whereby, within set limits, employees may begin and end work at times of their own choice'. It found that one in eight employers had introduced flexitime over the past three years and one in ten planned to introduce or increase its scope in the future. Flexitime is most common in public administration, banking, transport and communications.[1] One-quarter of respondents to the Jim Conway Foundation survey worked flexitime.[2]

The campaign for a 35-hour week

In April 1989, the Confederation of Shipbuilding and Engineering Unions – inspired by the success of the German engineers' union, I.G. Metall – launched its campaign to cut the working week from 39 to 35 hours. The first phase, designed to achieve a 37-hour week, began with a series of consultations to establish exactly what the members wanted.

The first message was that these industrial workers wanted real cuts in working hours, not a lower threshold for overtime payments. And second, they did not want a repeat of the 1979 negotiations where the introduction of a 39-hour week often took the form of twelve minutes off each day – six minutes morning and afternoon or, in the most absurd cases, three minutes' reduction at the start and end of each shift.

Two strategic conclusions emerged. First, the unions should press for a truly shorter working week, with an early finish on Fridays. As the AEEU's President, Bill Jordan, said: 'We are not talking about 10 minutes off each day. We are looking for the long weekend.'[3] Second, the cut in hours should be intimately linked with the more efficient organisation of work. Efficiency gains through new shift systems could not only help to finance the cost of reduced hours, but they also made it more difficult for managers to reinstate lengthy overtime.

In the words of Alex Ferry, general secretary of the Confederation, the first phase of the campaign succeeded 'beyond our wildest dreams'.[4] A £20-million campaign fund (of which £7 million remains available for the next phase) financed a series of strikes at selected workplaces, including key British Aerospace sites. By April 1991, 1,425 37-hour agreements had been reached, covering 600,000 workers.

Throughout the campaign, the emphasis on family issues was striking. Material sent to trades unionists stressed that the 35-hour was needed 'to give our members more time to spend with their families and to have more time for leisure', and quoted members saying: 'This will give me the time to actually enjoy my time with my family instead of spending all the time clearing up after them.' The family perspective united men and women workers: according to Ferry, the men were 'very keen' on the 4½ day week but the women were 'intense'!

Amongst the engineering workers featured in the campaign were a toolmaker able to use his extra time to help care for his five-year old boy who suffers from cerebral palsy, giving his wife some badly-needed time off; a machine-setter who managed to get extra fishing and more time with his children into his Friday afternoons; an electric assembler who uses her extra time to care for two house-bound elderly neighbours; and a fitter who devotes his Friday afternoons to tennis coaching of children. For some part-time workers, the shorter working week held out the prospect of moving to full-time work; for those already working full-time, it provided a breathing space 'to bank our wages, pay into the electricity or gas showrooms and do the shopping so that we have the weekends more free.'[5]

Engineering employers resisted the campaign, arguing that it would reduce competitiveness and cost jobs. But the early failure of BAe's legal challenge to industrial challenge encouraged management to turn their attention to winning new working methods. The Engineering Employers' Federation, for instance, argued the case for annual hours contracts to meet seasonal shifts in demand. In many agreements, the shorter working week was coupled with the elimination of rest breaks as well as greater functional flexibility within the workplace.

The timing of the next stage of the campaign to cut industrial workers' hours has not been decided. Clearly, the recession has had an effect on unions' estimate of their ability to win a further success. Just as the earlier move to a 39-hour basic week in engineering set a new pattern for manual workers, however, so the shorter working week has begun to be introduced in other industries.

In some cases, however, working hours are so long that even a substantial reduction will leave employees a long way above the 37-hour week. In the spring of 1992, for instance, British Rail offered employees a 41-hour week, with a further four hours at managers' discretion. This 45-hour week would have meant a reduction in the working week of 10 hours for craft shops, where the average week was 51 hours, and 22 hours in some depots with an average week of 63 hours.

An hour off a day, a day off a fortnight

A reduction in the basic working week can be distributed in several different ways. For instance, a reduction from 40 to 35 hours a week could be used as:

- an hour off each working day
- Friday afternoons off each week

- a 9-day fortnight

As we have seen, the British engineering workers insisted on a long weekend rather than a brief reduction in each working day. The unions' first agreement for a 37-hour week, with NEI Parsons in Newcastle, provided for a four and a half day week, with Friday finishing time moving from 1.20 p.m. to 12 midday over a period of eighteen months. Most later agreements followed a similar pattern. At Rolls Royce in Coventry and some other companies, however, the 37-hour week took the form of a nine-day fortnight.

Johnson Wax harmonised weekly hours for manual and non-manual workers at 37½, introducing a four and a half day week in 1985, with non-manual employees finishing at 1 p.m. on Fridays, manual employees at 12.30. Afternoon breaks which had previously operated for both groups were discontinued, as was the 'washing up' time for manual employees.

Even before the engineering workers' strike, nine-day fortnights had begun to make an appearance, particularly within local government. In the London Borough of Hillingdon, for instance, almost all officers work a nine-day fortnight, of eight hours a day, in which a 40-hour week alternates with a 32-hour week. 'Flexitime' also operates, giving staff some choice over the organisation of their working hours outside the 'core' times of 10 a.m. to midday and 2 p.m. to 4 p.m. The day taken off each fortnight – known as a 'flexiday' – can be chosen by each employee, provided that the section's work requirements are met. All employees are required to clock in and out in order that the working time operation can be controlled.[6]

Plants work longer than people

One of the benefits which flexitime offers employers is the opportunity to extend opening hours – and thus service to customers – without necessarily increasing individuals' working hours or taking on more staff. In manufacturing industry, 'decoupling' individuals' working hours from plant operating hours has similarly enabled employers to reduce the average working week while simultaneously achieving large productivity gains.

As a European Community report stresses, 'shortening operating hours can be expensive, and the modern trend is much more to lengthen operating hours for the organization, at the same time as giving employees shorter working hours. Then the only solution is "decoupling", disconnecting the link between the operating hours of the business and the working hours of the employee.[7]

For instance, in a landmark agreement reached with the TGWU, Michelin Tyres reduced the average working week for many of its shift workers in Burnley to 31½ hours through the introduction of a five-crew shift from January 1988.[8] Reduced hours were similarly achieved at Metal Box. At Westland Helicopters, a 32½-hour working week was negotiated on the basis of a move from day work to shift work and the introduction of computer-aided design and manufacturing (CAD/CAM) systems.[9]

At Michelin, workers were involved in extensive discussions about preferred shift patterns within the framework of continuous, 24-hour-a-day, seven-days-a-week production. The agreement was expected to create a substantial number of new jobs and also led to improved weekend shift premia, as well as annual pay rises staged over three years.

A move from four-crew to five-crew shiftworking can produce substantial gains for the enterprise, by extending operating hours and reducing the levels of contractual overtime. For employees, five-crew shiftworking may produce – as the Michelin, Westland and Metal Box examples show – a substantial reduction in the average working week. The new shiftworking pattern may also mean, however, that holiday breaks are integrated into the shift rota, thus reducing or removing any element of choice about when holidays are taken.

Where four-crew shiftworking remains, continuous operation can involve extremely long hours. For instance, four crews may work twelve hour shifts, with a cycle of day shifts, night shifts and rest days operating over four weeks or more. In such a case, a working week of 60 hours (five shifts and two rest days) may alternate with a working week of 24 hours (two shifts and five rest days). The gain in long blocks of leisure time must be set against the substantial disadvantages of long shifts, frequent night and weekend work and correspondingly disrupted social and family life.

'Decoupling' working and operating hours is, of course, widespread in the retail sector. But other companies have found it useful to stagger individuals' working time in order to make better use of expensive equipment. In Germany, for instance, one company achieved 12-hour use of its CAD equipment between two design engineers, one of whom worked from 6 a.m. to 2 p.m. and the other from 10 a.m. to 6 p.m.[10]

From full-time to part-time - and back again

'Full-time' and 'part-time' workers are usually seen as different people doing different jobs. Movement by full-timers into part-time work, and vice versa, remains rare.

In 1983, however, the Inland Revenue Staff Federation (IRSF) concluded a pioneering agreement on voluntary part-time working. Building on earlier agreements which covered officers experiencing temporary domestic problems and a limited number of long-serving staff in local offices, the agreement allows any Inland Revenue officer who has completed the probationary period to apply for part-time working.

In deciding whether or not to grant the application, managers have to consider the operational needs of the office, existing opportunities for part-time work and the possibility of creating new part-time opportunities, possibly on a job-sharing basis. Priority is given to women and men who want to reduce their hours of work in order to look after children, or sick or elderly relatives, or to cope with a domestic crisis. The possibility of part-time working as a prelude to retirement is also specifically mentioned.

The Inland Revenue agreement indicates that, as far as possible, managers will meet the applicant's preference about working patterns and hours of attendance. Pay, holiday and sick leave entitlement for those moving to part-time jobs will be the appropriate proportion of full-time conditions; pension scheme membership is retained. Where part-time working is authorised for a specific period, the officer retains a right to return to full-time working. In other cases, there is no automatic right to return to full-time duties, although managers retain a discretion to accept such an application. Furthermore, if the situation in the office changes, an officer who has moved to part-time working may be required, with at least three months' notice, to return to full-time work.

This agreement represents an imaginative compromise between the Inland Revenue's need for staffing flexibility in order to deal with seasonal variations in its work, the trade union's concern about the possible employment of casual and temporary labour and its desire to meet members' preferences about working time changes. Over 7,000 people in a workforce of 60,000 have taken advantage of the opportunity to reduce their hours.

The first Inland Revenue agreement on voluntary part-time working applied to *existing* full-time officers. A further agreement in July 1989 allowed for the *recruitment* of permanent, part-time officers. The agreement makes it clear that part-time working will not be confined to any specific job or area of work; instead, jobs will be advertised as open to people wishing to work full-time or part-time. *Pro rata* terms and conditions of employment, as specified in the earlier agreement, will apply to officers recruited part-time, who will also be entitled to move to full-time working at any stage if appropriate vacancies exist. In January 1991, further agreement was reached on the possibility of part-year (including term-time) working. The impact of the first two agreements is now under joint review by management and unions.

Shorter working hours at the employee's initiative may also be introduced through V-time ('voluntary reduced time' schemes). V-time allows full-time employees to reduce their working hours, with corresponding loss of pay, for a specified period. The reduction in hours is temporary, and return to full-time work is guaranteed. For instance, in a pilot V-time scheme, the Alliance and Leicester Building Society allows full-time employees with children aged between 5 and 14 to opt to take time off during the school holidays.

The British Civil Service

The Inland Revenue is only one of several government departments which have encouraged the development of shorter hours working. Following a review of employment opportunities for women in the early 1980s, an action programme was agreed between civil service management and unions in 1984. Departments were urged to expand opportunities for part-time work and to give 'sympathetic consideration' to staff requests for part-time posts. Job-sharing experiments were to be established and special unpaid leave (for instance, to cover school holidays or deal with family crises) more widely publicised.[11]

In 1989, the Council of Civil Service Unions reached an agreement with the Treasury about alternative working patterns within the Civil Service, including the use of annual hours contracts. The agreement confirmed that, although the traditional full-time career will remain the norm for the foreseeable future, 'more varied approaches to patterns of work' will enable the Civil Service to respond both to technological changes and to the desire of many staff for flexibility in their work. Thus, 'regardless of the pattern of working, all staff should have fair and open opportunities for career development, including promotion and training and be able to move between patterns at different stages in their career'.

The following year, the government published a brochure for civil servants, *Made to Measure*, describing the range of part-time and job-sharing opportunities available and stressing the benefits to management as well as staff. Part-time staff are guaranteed the same pay scales, annual leave allowances and annual increments, on a *pro rata* basis, as full-time employees. Promotion and training opportunities are, in theory, equally open to them, although the 1991 review found that actual promotion rates were lower for women than for men, and lower for women working part-time than for those working full-time. Civil servants recruited to part-time work, or who move from full-time to part-time work, are not generally guaranteed a right to move to full-time work, although managers are expected to agree such requests where possible.

By 1991, the proportion of women civil servants working part-time had trebled, from under 5% to over 14%. (Since only 1% of men work part-time, the overall proportion of part-time civil servants is around 7%.) Women and part-time employees continue to be concentrated in the lower grades. Half of all civil servants are women, but women make up only 7% of Grades 2 and there are only two women Permanent Secretaries. There are now four part-time civil servants at Under Secretary level (Grade 3), including the head of personnel in the Department of Social Security and the principal finance officer in the property holdings section of the Department of Environment. Thirty-one women at Grade 5 now work part-time (one in eight of all women at this grade), as do ten men.[12] With women representing about one in eight of senior middle management, there is the prospect of more women – and more part-timers – being promoted to top posts over the next decade.

Civil servants in other countries

In most other industrialised countries, civil servants are entitled by law to work part-time in a wide variety of permanent, career posts.

Table 2.1 summarises the civil service programmes available in other countries. (These apply to national or federal civil servants; in some countries, more generous provisions apply to those employed by state governments.)

There are several important points to note about the treatment of part-time working in the civil services of these countries. First, part-time working is usually voluntary. The exception is Belgium which introduced compulsory part-time working, at 80% of normal hours, in the first year of employment for all civil servants recruited after the end of 1983. This measure was part of a programme designed to reduce unemployment as well as public expenditure. In one of the German Lander, Lower Saxony, the ILO found that all new civil servants were required to accept part-

Table 2.1: Part-time opportunities for civil servants

Country	Eligibility	Hours	Pay/conditions	Return to full-time	Duration
Australia	All with 3 mths service	15–30	*Pro rata*	Right to return after agreed period	By agreement
Austria	Women with children 1–4 All caring for close relative	Half-time	–	Ditto	1 or 2 yrs; 4 yrs total
Belgium	Permanent civil servants with family/social needs; for personal convenience	50%–80% normal hrs	*Pro rata*	Ditto	3 mths–2 yrs at one time; 5 yrs total
Canada	All	Minimum ⅓ normal hrs	*Pro rata*	–	–
France	All	50%–90% normal hrs	*Pro rata*	Ditto	6 mths minimum
Germany	All with child below 18 or dependent adult	Minimum 50% normal hrs	–	With permission	Up to 15 yrs
Italy	All; limit on total part-time posts	Minimum 50% normal hrs	*Pro rata*	–	–
Luxembourg	All with child below 15 or 'well-motivated' personal reasons; very senior posts excluded	Half-time	*Pro rata* for pensions; does not count towards promotion	Only if full-time vacancy	No limit
New Zealand	All, for personal reasons	–	*Pro rata*	–	–
Portugal	All with 3 yrs service, with children under 12, sick relative or educational needs; except directorate or executive positions	Half-time	*Pro rata*	Right to return on request	6 mths; can be extended
Sweden	All	Compatible with service	*Pro rata*	–	No limit
USA	All up to grade GS-16	16–32 hrs	*Pro rata*	–	–

'-' indicates no information given

Source: *Conditions of Work Digest: Part-time work*, Geneva, International Labour Office, 1989.

time employment at three-quarters of their normal hours; another Land dropped similar ideas after complaints by the civil service union.

Second, provision is made in most cases for full-time workers who have reduced their hours to return to full-time working in the same or equivalent job. In some cases, return to full-time work is automatic after the end of the agreed period for part-time work; in others, the employer has to agree to the employee's request. Where no provision is made for a move to full-time work, this is usually because the employee has been recruited on a part-time basis.

Third, in almost every civil service, the pay and conditions of part-time workers are equivalent to those of full-timers. Pay, sick pay, pension and holiday entitlement are *pro rata* to the proportion of full-time hours worked; promotion and seniority rights are usually preserved.

Fourth, attempts are made to treat part-time work as an integral part of the career pattern. For instance, the New South Wales public service in Australia treats part-time work as 'an integral part of the public employment system' and makes it available to all occupational categories and levels except for departmental heads. In the USA – not widely regarded as a model for the treatment of parents – all federal agencies are required to establish programmes to expand part-time career employment opportunities, with annual goals and time-tables, and twice-yearly reports to the Office of Personnel Management. In Germany, after two years of the new legal provisions, the ILO found that the number of part-time federal civil servants had increased rapidly to nearly one in five of the total.

Part-time work for new parents

Many of the civil service schemes described above make special provision for employees returning after maternity, paternity or parental leave. In 1984, a Home Office civil servant, Ms Holmes, who had been refused part-time employment after her maternity leave ended, successfully sued for indirect sex discrimination.[13] Despite insisting at the time on the 'special circumstances' of the case, the civil service – although not guaranteeing a right to return part-time – now makes it much easier for new parents to do so. *Made to Measure* gives the example of a woman working at senior (Grade 5) level, who returned to work part-time after the birth of her first child and was promoted as a part-timer. It also quotes a male Higher Executive Officer, working three days a week as a job-sharer, who divides childcare responsibilities with his wife, who also works part-time.

Several other countries have created a legal right for employees to move to part-time employment while a child is young. Sweden guarantees eighteen months' paid parental leave, with father and mother able to share the leave between them and to take part or all of the leave part-time. In addition, parents have the right to work a six-hour day, with loss of pay but without losing employment security, until the child reaches the age of eight or completes the first year of schooling. Indeed, the combination of time off for parenthood, family leave, trade union activities and further training mean that much part-time work in Sweden is not because employers have created part-time jobs, but arises from individuals' decisions to reduce full-time work.[14]

In Finland since 1988, one parent at a time can work part-time (six hours a day, 30 hours a week) until the child reaches the age of four and during the child's first term of schooling. In France, a law of 1984 allows any employee with at least one year's employment before the birth or adoption of a child to work half-time until the child's third birthday. (The *ecoles maternelles* cater for children from the age of three.) Employers with 100 or more employees cannot refuse a parent's request to work half-time. Smaller employers can refuse such a request if it would be 'prejudicial to the production and running of the company', but must first consult with the works council or staff representatives; a refusal may be appealed to an industrial tribunal. A parent working half-time receives 50% of normal pay and half-time employment is treated in the same way as full-time employment for seniority purposes.[15]

Greece permits mothers with a child under two to request two hours' less work per day without loss of pay, and allows any employee with a dependant to work one hour less each day (with loss of pay). Portugal also allows breastfeeding mothers to work one hour less each day without losing pay.[16]

Part-time working before retirement

Part-time working before retirement is also guaranteed by law in several industrialised countries. Since 1987, Denmark has allowed people between the age of 60 and 67 (the national retirement age) to move from full-time to part-time work, and obtain a partial pension in return. Those taking part-time retirement can reduce their hours by up to nine a week, or one-quarter of their previous average, but must continue to work between 15 and 39 hours a week Finland allows employees aged between 60 and 65 to reduce their weekly working hours to between 16 and 28 and to draw a partial pension in addition to their part-time earnings.

Sweden introduced a similar scheme in 1979, which proved so popular that the conditions for entitlement had to be made more restrictive.[17]

In Germany, the Older Workers Part-time Act came into effect at the beginning of 1989, replacing provisions for early retirement with an entitlement to half-time work before retirement. Any full-time worker aged between 58 and 65 (the normal retirement age) can apply for part-time work. Employers are only obliged to accept such applications if part-time working is covered by collective or workplace agreements and need only extend part-time working to 5% of their employees. Small firms, with under 20 employees, are not required to participate in the scheme. Half-time older workers must work at least 18 hours a week. In addition to their half-pay, they receive a further 20% of their part-time pay, which is not subject to income tax or social security contributions. If the employer recruits unemployed workers to make up the part-time worker's hours, he can claim back the 20% wage subsidy from the state.[18]

Part-time working to create new jobs

In France, half-time employment for older workers is also promoted as a means of creating additional jobs. Full-time employees aged between 55 and 60 may move to part-time employment under agreements signed between the government and the employer, following consultation with employees' representatives. A new employee must be hired within three months of the existing full-timer's move to phased retirement. New employees may be hired full-time or part-time (for instance, two part-timers can be hired to compensate for two full-timers going part-time). The part-time older worker receives a government grant of 30% of their full-time salary up to a specified limit, in addition to the half-time salary.

In a similar scheme in Spain, the Workers' Charter of 1980 provides half-time work and a half pension for workers aged between 62 and 65, provided an unemployed replacement is hired for at least the period up until the original worker's retirement age. In 1986, only just over 1,000 'replacement contracts' were registered.

In Belgium, throughout the 1980s, the Government has experimented with more general measures to reduce working hours and promote part-time work as a path to job creation. Since 1985, employees who have been with their organisation for at least a year have been entitled to take career breaks with the agreement of their employer, or on the basis of a collective agreement. Career leave may be taken full-time or half-time and the person on leave must be replaced by a registered unemployed person. Someone taking half-time leave receives, in addition to their half-pay, a monthly state benefit during their leave for up to five years (for employees under 50) or until retirement age (for older workers).

In Britain, the part-time job release scheme was designed to create jobs for the unemployed by encouraging people near retirement age to work part-time. The Jobshare scheme, which developed from the job-splitting scheme introduced in 1983, enabled employers to convert full-time posts into two part-time jobs, or to create new part-time jobs in place of a full-time post; provided the new employees were recruited from the unemployment register or other specified groups, the employer received a grant of £1,000. The scheme had little impact: the ILO reported that between 1983 and March 1987, only 1,654 applications for support were approved. In October 1991, the government announced that the scheme would be wound up.

Job-sharing

Job-sharing is a variation on part-time work, where two employees share a single job, often deciding between them the arrangement of working hours. For instance, job-sharers may work one week on, one week off; one may work mornings, the other afternoons; they may work alternate days, or divide the days between them in some other way.

The ACAS survey in 1987 found that 10% of employers had introduced job-sharing over the previous three years; 8% planned to introduce it, or to increase its scope. Job sharing is most common amongst white-collar employees in banking, local government and other public administration, where over one-third of those surveyed had introduced it.[19] A survey in the same year by the job-sharers' organisation, New Ways to Work, found 56 local authorities with formal job sharing policies, employing over 2,000 job sharers.[20] Within the civil service, job-sharing is fairly widely available, with two job-sharing appointments at Grade 5.

The CBI also reports the example of a British food and drink manufacturing company which introduced job sharing into its production process, in the form of shorter shifts. They quote an executive in the firm:

> Job sharing has been a great success story in one of our subsidiaries.
> . . . Once we introduced continuous process production we found
> that five hour shifts coincided with the optimum length of our
> production runs. Given that greater flexibility became necessary due
> to the proliferation of differing packaging requirements, shorter

shift work facilitated maximum employee mobility. So we introduced job sharing – and we haven't looked back. . . . We have increased employment by 100% and some 75% of our employees in the packing areas are covered by job sharing. . . . We can produce what we want when we want. We haven't encountered any disadvantages yet. We were worried about rising administration costs. But as we computerised our wage payments systems at the same time, we've had no problems.[21]

Longer working days/longer time off

Even if overall hours are unaltered, more flexible working arrangements make it possible to trade off a longer working day against longer blocks of leisure time. A 40-hour week could, for instance, be worked as four 10-hour days with a three-day weekend; a 36-hour week could be worked as four 9-hour days with a three-day weekend or as three 12-hour days with a four-day 'weekend'. Or working time could be reorganised over a longer period. For instance, a 40-hour week (160-hour month) could be reorganised into three, six-day weeks of just under nine hours a day, with a full week off every month.

Longer blocks of leisure time are generally favoured by employees. (A detailed discussion of employees' working time preferences will be found in chapter 4.) But working longer days in return may cause problems. Trades unions are generally reluctant to allow a departure from the basic eight-hour day, which was won with such difficulty earlier this century. Depending on the nature of the work, a significantly longer day may lead to lower productivity (tired workers are less efficient) as well as greater stress and other health problems amongst employees.

Nonetheless, Britain is starting to see arrangements which trade a longer working day for longer periods of time off. In 1985, the TGWU reached an agreement with a London engineering company for a 35-hour week worked over four days. The chief engineer was reported as saying that: 'We can run four longer days more efficiently'.[22]

The three-day working week during the miners' strike in 1973 demonstrated vividly that a week's work did not necessarily take a week. A survey of flexible working patterns by the Institute of Personnel Management found that one company, which had maintained its five-day output during the three-day week, then moved to a four-day, ten-hours a day pattern. Overhead costs (including heating and lighting) fell, overtime was virtually eliminated, output improved, and the company found it easier to recruit and retain people.[23]

In 1989, British Coal proposed six-day working in order to increase the use of capital equipment in new mines and existing mines where major reconstruction is to take place. The proposal was bitterly rejected by the National Union of Mineworkers (NUM) who saw it as part of a wider strategy to close a number of pits and to abolish the statutory seven and a half-hour limit on shift length.[24] So far, six-day working only operates at Asfordby, where individual miners work the same annual number of hours as those employed in five-day pits, on the basis of three six-day weeks followed by one week off. The NUM has refused to negotiate arrangements for 6-day weeks, and the new pit at Margam in South Wales, where British Coal intended to introduce the new scheme, has not so far been developed.

Longer blocks of time off may also be provided as part of an agreement to reduce working hours, if the existing working week remains unchanged. In 1980, the National Union of Journalists (NUJ) reached a national agreement to reduce the working hours of provincial journalists from 80 to 75 per fortnight. On the *Yorkshire Post*, journalists continued to work the same shifts as before, with a 40-hour week, but 'banked' their five extra hours each fortnight in the form of 17 additional days off each year. By arrangement with managers, days off can be taken singly or consecutively. In this way, the enterprise avoided the introduction of complex shift patterns which a 37½-hour week would have entailed.[25]

In a similar arrangement, Massey Ferguson in Coventry operate a time bank scheme to bridge the gap between the contractual 39-hour week and the actual 40-hour week which is worked. The time banked can be taken as extra holidays or used to facilitate earlier retirement on full pension.[26]

Term-time jobs

Term-time employment has long been preferred by many women with children, either because they are unable to find holiday care or because they positively want to share time with their families. Indeed, this is one of the reasons for the concentration of women in teaching and other educational jobs. But other organisations are beginning to understand the value of term-time employment in recruiting and retaining women. Boots the Chemist, for instance, has been offering term-time contracts for several years. The company also offers term-time employees additional work during the school holiday period, an option that has proved popular.

Like many other retailers seeking to improve recruitment and extend opening hours, the DIY chain, B&Q, introduced term-time employment in 1990, offering a 40-week year with the salary spread evenly across the twelve months of the year. The technicalities of employment law make it important for term-time workers to be paid continuously, rather than risking an interruption in their contract and continuity of employment with every school holiday.

Weekend jobs

The growth in consumer demand for services at weekends, and the extension of Sunday trading has led to the creation of some 'weekend jobs'.

The National Communications Union, for instance, has negotiated an agreement with the Post Office to allow a 22-hour working week concentrated into the weekends. The short hours, starting at 3.30 p.m. on Friday and ending at 7 a.m. on Monday, will involve two shifts of no more than 12 hours each. This arrangement will only be available for part of the year, probably between April and July, and will depend on workloads.[27] Another British example is given in the case study of the DIY firm, B&Q (see p.50 below).

In Belgium, following a liberalisation of the law on working time, some companies have created weekend-only jobs. These involve long shifts – 12 hours – on Saturday and Sunday, for which employees are paid the rate for a full 36-hour week. Research reported to the European Foundation for the Improvement of Living and Working Conditions indicates that 'some workers are happy – at least for the time being – to concentrate their work on two days and have five days to do other things, while others complain that their family life and social contacts are jeopardised, as well as possibilities for engaging in cultural or recreational activities.'[28]

In France, the car manufacturing company, Regie Renault, reached an agreement with the trade unions in 1985 to establish weekend jobs. Weekend work is filled by volunteers from the permanent workforce and lasts for a period of three months which may be renewed. They work ten hours on Saturday and on Sunday, with a further eight hours on Friday or Monday. Wage rates are fixed in such a way that the pay for the 28-hour weekend work is slightly higher than that for a normal working week.

The three-day weekend is treated as equivalent to a full week for the calculation of holidays and sick pay.[29]

Annual hours contracts

The desire of many employers to match the workforce more closely to peaks and troughs in demand and, thus, to increase competitiveness has in some cases to the use of 'annual hours contracts'. Whereas the traditional contract of employment specifies a basic or normal working week, an annual hours contract specifies the total number of hours over an entire year. Thus, a 40-hour week, with five weeks' holidays, would become an annual contract for 1,880 hours; a 35-hour week with five weeks' holidays is equivalent to an annual contract for 1,645 hours. Since the advantage of an annual hours contract is, however, that the hours are not necessarily the same from week to week, the contract may also specify the pattern of working over the year, or give managers considerable discretion in deciding the individual's working pattern.

The ACAS survey in 1987 found that only 3% of companies had introduced annual hours working in the previous three years, although 8% planned to introduce it or increase its scope. More recently, only 3% of respondents to the Equal Opportunities Commission survey reported that their hours were set annually; most of these worked in education, where over a quarter of employees had annual hours contracts. Informal arrangements were more common in meeting the demand for seasonal flexibility.[30]

Annual hours contracts have been used, for instance, by some local councils in their parks and gardens service. The demand for additional staffing in the summer months and less in the winter months, could in principle be met in a variety of ways. A 'core' of permanent staff could be supplemented by casual labour during the summer, or could themselves be required to work long overtime hours for part of the year. With annual hours contracts, the total demand for staffing throughout the year can be met by the permanent workforce, whose weekly hours will vary considerably depending on the time of year. If overtime payments are reduced substantially, as is frequently the case with an annual hours contract, and if there is no increase in basic pay to compensate, individuals' earnings will suffer. On the other hand, the permanent workforce may be larger than it would otherwise have been since the demand for additional staffing in the summer is no longer being met by casual workers.

In November 1990, manual workers at Hotpoint voted to accept a shorter working week package, involving longer hours in the first seven months of the year and shorter hours for the remaining five. The new arrangements were designed to meet seasonal demand for domestic appliances.[31]

A similar seasonal pattern is found within ICI Agrochemicals. Incomes Data Services reports that: 'A centrally negotiated agreement on a 2½ hour reduction in the working week gave ICI Agrochemicals the opportunity to match working time to the seasonal nature of demand and production.' The reduced working week of 37½ hours was divided between 40 hours a week in the first six months of the year, and 35 hours a week in the second six months. Employees are paid for a 37½ hour week throughout the year; overtime continues to be worked in the busier period, but the threshold for overtime premia remains 40 hours.[32]

In May 1991, management and unions in the ICI Group agreed a comprehensive package of pay rises, harmonisation of manual and white-collar conditions, cuts in hours and reorganisation of working time within the framework of annual hours.[33] From 1993, working hours will be cut to 1633.6 a year – equivalent to an average 36-hour working week – on condition that local agreement could be reached on 'the effective organisation of working hours and patterns of work to ensure the best utilisation of time with minimal recourse to overtime working'. The introduction to the agreement recognised the 'mutual agreement' that ICI's businesses needed to work continuously to achieve international competitiveness and stressed the need for 'personal and career develop-ment', with regular training and broader educational opportunities throughout each employee's working life. In this case, the re-organisation of working time was central to a strategy designed to improve com-petitiveness by upgrading manual workers.

The need to match operating hours more closely to customer demand was the motive behind the introduction of annualized hours by Bristol and West Building Society. In February 1991, staff were offered contracts for 1,826 hours a year with optional overtime 'packages' of 175 hours each. Although the building society said that its main aim was not to cut overtime costs, but to provide the flexible staffing needed to vary opening hours, the banking union, BIFU, feared that the new contracts would reduce some employees' overtime payments.[34]

Within the paper industry, a national agreement which came into effect in 1983 allowed local employers and trade unions either to reduce working hours through annual hours contracts or to reduce manual workers' hours by 47 per year by other means.

Wiggins Teape, a major European pulp and paper group, followed the agreement by introducing annual hours at its semi-continuous production plant, Stowford Mill, at Ivybridge. Previously, manual employees had worked a three-crew system with three eight-hour shifts; five weeks' annual holiday were provided, including a 10-day annual shutdown and three days at Christmas. Under the annual hours arrangements, shifts are rotated over six weeks, with the seventh week taken off completely. The afternoon shift involves a 40-hour week; the morning shift (which includes Saturday morning) 46 hours; and the night shift 48 hours. Employees receive seven leisure weeks in addition to the two-week summer shutdown and the one-week Christmas shutdown. The increase from five to ten weeks off a year corresponds to a reduction in the working week by 4½ hours. Earnings have been maintained at their previous level, with the reduction in overtime opportunities compensated for by higher weekly earnings (which are equalised throughout the working year).

The benefits of such a system are obvious: more leisure, shorter average weekly working hours and no loss in earnings. There is, however, no choice about when leisure weeks are taken and the night shift (two weeks out of every six) still involves a long working week. From the point of view of the enterprise, absenteeism levels have been reduced and operating hours maintained.[35]

Absorbing holiday entitlements within annual hours contracts may also enable enterprises to extend the operating year. For instance, IDS found that Don & Low, a Scottish-based industrial textiles manufacturer, had previously closed down at Christmas and in the spring, summer and autumn in order to accommodate six weeks' annual holidays for shiftworkers. As a result, the 'production year' was 46.4 weeks. With annual hours working, although the Christmas shutdown has been retained, the production year has been extended to 50.7 weeks as other holiday entitlements, together with other rest days, have been rostered within the shift rota. The new working arrangements, which were developed and negotiated over 18 months, succeeded in meeting the employees' and unions' preference for more leisure time without a loss of earnings, and managers' objectives of a longer production year, the retention of the 168-hour operating week and no rise in unit costs.

IBM UK has combined annual hours contracts with the introduction of part-time working for a small, but growing proportion of its staff. In order to improve the return on its substantial investment in high-technology training, IBM sought to increase the number of women returning to work after taking maternity leave. The strategy of 'career breaks' pursued by a number of financial services companies (see below, p.48) is inappropriate in a sector where skills must be updated almost continuously.

Instead, IBM sought to match working hours to the needs of women with very young children. A woman wanting to return part-time is, therefore, employed on an annual hours contract which specifies the total number of hours to be worked over the year and which provides, on a *pro rata* basis, the same terms and conditions as a permanent full-time worker. Within the overall number of hours, the departmental manager has the discretion to agree a working pattern which suits both the employee and the project on which she is working. Managers' abilities to plan ahead for a project and the need to adjust to a pressure of demand which builds up towards the end of each year has enabled many women on an annual hours contract to work during school terms only, as well as working a shorter week and/or day than usual.

Annualised hours, however, do not always work to the benefits of employees. Within the broadcasting industry, intense competitive pressures have led many companies to demand the kind of flexibility which makes family life impossible. An ITN floor manager, for instance, found her three-day-a-week job-share translated into a 900 hours annual contract which, in practice, required her to be on call every day, without advance warning. Since childcare was impossible to plan, she had no alternative but to take redundancy.[36]

Zero hours contracts

A zero hours contract is a legal device which avoids the need to specify the number of hours to be worked weekly, monthly or annually and instead requires the employee to work 'as and when required'. 'On call' arrangements, such as those used by the civil service, enable the employer to offer work when it is needed with little or no notice, but do not require the person on call to accept it.

The Equal Opportunities Commission survey of employees was unable to find any example of a zero hours contract, although it did find significant minorities of full-time and part-time employees who were 'on call' outside their contracted hours.[37] The parallel survey of employers included a social services department which used 'no fixed hours' contracts to help meet the changing demands for community care.[38]

Zero hours contracts usually leave employees without statutory legal protection. For instance, a woman bank clerk was employed for 35 hours in one week and zero hours in the next week; when she was made redundant, her employers paid a redundancy payment based on continuous service, but were refused the government rebate on the grounds that the continuity had been broken with each 'zero hours' week.[39]

Individual working hours

The introduction of a shorter working week, possibly combined with annual hours contracts, can serve both employees and employers. They do not necessarily, however, accommodate the varying needs of different employees. Individual choice of working hours may offer greater benefits.

As *Made to Measure* stresses, the British civil service is now offering a range of flexible working patterns to part-time staff, who can work any number or arrangement of hours. A part-time civil servant may, for instance, work a regular two, three or four day week, or work school hours daily, or combine two full days with three days which end at 2.30 p.m. so that children can be collected from school. Term-time working is used, for instance by the Lord Chancellor's Department to help cover busier periods in courts, but is not widely established.

In Norway, it is now common for hospitals and other large organisations to offer employees a choice about the *number* of hours worked and *when* they are worked. The staffing needs of different sections of the hospital at different times of the week are matched, using information technology, with the preferences of employees. Overtime payments and premia for antisocial hours allow individuals to make their own trade-off between time and money. The requirements of the hospital are met in a system which also meets the working time preferences of most employees.

Similar arrangements are also becoming more common in the retail sector in Germany. For instance, Modehaus Beck, a Munich department store, gives its 700 employees, most of them women, a choice of average monthly hours ranging from 60 to 170. The hours of work are agreed at the beginning of each month in accordance with each department's monthly sales plan; a more detailed weekly plan is worked out by each department head. Sales assistants, who receive a commission on sales, have annual time contracts but can choose when to work; for obvious reasons, most choose to work at peak shopping times when more sales are made than at slack periods. Thus, employees are able to make their own time-money trade-offs while still meeting the needs of the enterprise. The company reports that the scheme has been extremely successful since the number of staff can be matched to customers, and staff are more highly motivated. An offer to return to normal working hours after a trial period of two years was rejected by the employees.

Another German company, Karstadt AG, employs over 60,000 people in its 161 department stores. A scheme for flexible working hours has been agreed with the works council at company level and combined with the introduction of computing systems to manage working time arrangements. Again, employees can choose their working hours, varying between 75 a month (the threshold for social security payments) and 167 a month (normal full-time hours). The length and arrangement of each individual's working hours are fixed at least two weeks, and normally four weeks, in advance. Pay and all benefits are paid *pro rata* to employees on shorter hours; training is available to part-timers on the same terms as full-timers; and employees wanting to change from full-time to shorter hours working, and vice versa, have priority over external candidates when vacancies arise.[40]

The development of a wide variety of non-standard working time arrangements has also been particularly marked in the British retailing sector. The case-study on page 50 illustrates the variety and complexity of working time arrangements which can already be found within a single organisation.

It might appear difficult for shift systems in manufacturing to accommodate people who wished to work a variety of hours. There are, however, some examples of individual working time arrangements in industry.

Over ten years ago, the Volvo components company in Sweden, introduced a system of multiple and flexible working hours for its 3,000+ employees. The change was motivated by the need to meet the changing needs of the market at short notice, as well as by the demand for part-time work, particularly from women, and social pressures to employ more women. Management negotiated with the trades unions a complex scheme under which eight different kinds of schedules (full-time and part-time, shift, night and weekend work) could be combined in different ways according to production needs and, to a considerable extent, the preferences of employees. At union insistence, night and weekend work is performed only by volunteers, who have the right at short notice to return to their former working hours. The new arrangements enabled Volvo Komponenten to increase its competitiveness through better use of its more expensive equipment.

Time off during the working lifetime

In addition to changing patterns of daily, weekly and annual hours, further innovations are taking place which change the pattern of the working lifetime.

Leave for parents

The 1975 Employment Protection Act introduced a statutory right to eighteen weeks' paid maternity leave (6 weeks at 90% of full pay, the remainder at a low, flat-rate level) together with a right for women who had taken maternity leave to return to their previous employment for up to 29 weeks after the baby's birth.

A succession of changes to the qualifying conditions for maternity leave and reinstatement meant that, by 1990, nearly half of new mothers in employment did not qualify for these benefits. Some employers do, of course, offer longer paid maternity leave than the statutory minimum and/or extend it to women who would not qualify under the statutory scheme; but such arrangements are far more common in the public than in the private sector.[41]

Statutory entitlement to paid maternity leave is now much higher in most other European Community countries. For instance, women in Denmark are entitled to 28 weeks' leave on 90% of earnings; in Germany to 14 weeks on 100% of earnings; in France to 16 weeks on 90% of earnings; and in Italy to 20 weeks on 80% of earnings.[42] The proposal by the European Commission for a Directive on Parental Leave and Leave for Family Reasons has been blocked by the British government.

There is no statutory provision in Britain for paternity leave. Most fathers do, however, take one or two weeks' holiday at the time of their child's birth.[43]

Career breaks

Since 1981, career breaks have been introduced by a number of large employers, initially in banking and later in other financial and public sector institutions. Most such schemes provide for women (and, in theory at least, men) to take up to five years' unpaid leave after the end of paid maternity leave, with a right to return to work at the same grade afterwards. The employee remains in contact with the enterprise; in the banks, for instance, someone on a career break is required to work for two weeks a year, and to attend one or more one-day courses.

In general, career break schemes are available only to employees in management grades or with 'management potential' who have been with the organisation for a specified time. In one bank studied by Rapoport and Moss, however, there is a 'reservist' scheme under which lower level employees may take a career break; although the bank does not guarantee to re-employ them, it makes every effort to do so.

In another large bank interviewed for the same study, the scheme initially introduced in 1986 was extended two years later, so that 30,000 out of 85,000 staff are now eligible. Two breaks of up to two years each may be taken, with at least one year's full-time employment in between. Alternatively, an employee may apply to work part-time for up to two years after the end of maternity leave; she retains the same grade as before, but may be required to move to a different location or carry out different duties.

A recently privatised public utility covered by the same study offered two years' career break for senior employees, a 'reservist' scheme for other staff and the possibility for any employee to negotiate a new contract with flexible full-time or part-time hours after maternity leave ended. In this case, however, male employees are only eligible if their partner also works for the company (a provision which would appear to be vulnerable to challenge under the Sex Discrimination Act.)[44]

Sabbaticals

Sabbaticals – a paid year off in every seven – have long featured in the contracts of some senior, tenured academics. They are now beginning to appear elsewhere.

For instance, the John Lewis group has introduced six-month sabbaticals for employees aged 50 or over who had at least 25 years' service with the company. Sabbatical leave is available at all levels within the group, although people in specialist and senior management posts are required to give longer notice than other employees. Their absence is covered by the appointment of a trainee, or by re-organising colleagues' responsibilities. Thus, other employees have an opportunity to take on new responsibilities which can contribute to their personal and career development.[45]

A case-study of flexible working time: B&Q

B&Q, which is part of the Kingfisher group, is a major DIY chain, with 279 stores in Britain. In addition to its main administrative headquarters, it has five regional offices. 55% of its 15,000 employees are women; 96% of all employees work in stores. The majority of employees – 55% – are permanent part-timers, 70% of whom are women. Most of the remainder – 43% – are permanent full-timers, of whom nearly two-thirds are men. There are also a small number of temporary part-time and full-time workers (with more taken on during the summer). B&Q is not unionised.

Although women and men are equally represented amongst the sales floor staff (the majority of B&Q employees) and amongst head office staff, the majority of store managers, departmental managers, supervisors and consultants are men; the majority of store-based administrative staff are women. All store managers and almost all head office staff, departmental managers, supervisors and sales consultants work full-time; a majority of store-based administrative staff and most sales floor staff work part-time.

The standard working week for full-time employees outside the stores is 37½ hours and for full-time store staff 39 hours. A 'part-timer' in this company is anyone working below this level. Store staff work on a rota from Monday to Friday, Monday to Saturday or, in Scotland, where Sunday trading is legal, Monday to Sunday.

Part-time employees within B&Q work any of the following different patterns: Saturdays only; Sunday only; term-time only; mornings only; lunch-times only; afternoons only; evenings only.

Sixteen per cent of the total workforce (2,400 employees) work Saturdays only, fairly evenly divided between women and men. A further 14% work Sundays only, with 64% being women. Only 27 employees, all women, work in term-times only. The actual hours of other part-time workers vary according to the needs of the store and individual circumstances: for instance, a 'morning only' worker may work from 8 to 12, from 9 to 12, from 9 to 1, from 9 to 2 or a combination of these hours in each week. One store alone operates 34 different working time rotas.

Terms and conditions

B&Q pays its part-time employees the same basic hourly rate as full-timers. There is a complex system of qualification for other benefits.

Whereas all employees receive a company bonus and profit share regardless of hours, holiday pay is only available to those working at least 9 hours a week. Only those working 16 hours a week or more qualify for pension scheme membership, while 18 hours a week or more is required for sick pay (above the statutory minimum). Reflecting statutory provisions, maternity leave is available to those working between 8 and 16 hours if they have at least five years' service, and to those working 16 hours or more if they have at least two years' service.

Contractual overtime is limited to the twice-a-year stocktake and other special circumstances, such as a store conversion. Voluntary overtime is kept to a minimum. The increase in part-time employment – including weekend-only employment – has increased the number of Monday-to-Friday jobs and reduced the need for full-timers to work overtime, including at weekends.

A company survey of B&Q employees in August 1988 reported a high level of satisfaction amongst part-timers with their working hours; they felt under less pressure than full-timers and were less likely to be looking for another job. The results are consistent with other, wider surveys (see chapter 4).

3 THE SECOND SHIFT: WORK IN THE HOME

Most studies of work and working time pay little attention to unpaid work in the home. It is not measured by the national accounts. Far more information is available about how much time people spend working for money than about how much time they spend in housework, cooking, shopping, washing and looking after children and other dependent relatives. Oakley's investigation of housework nearly twenty years ago remains the most comprehensive account.[1]

Studies of women's work over several decades have, however, stressed women's double burden and the connections between their paid and unpaid work.[2] The extra demands placed upon women by home and family make it impossible for them to compete on equal terms with men in the workplace. Thus, the division of responsibilities between women and men at home directly affects the division of opportunities between women and men in employment. Because paid work has first claim on men's time, it restricts the time left for their families; because the family has first claim on women's time, it restricts the time left for paid work.

We have already seen that employed women – even those with full-time jobs – spend less time in paid work than employed men (p.11 above). In this section, I look at the time which women and men spend in unpaid work and the ways in which this division of time is also changing.

In the early 1970s, the sociologists Young and Wilmott studied the division of labour within the home. Rather optimistically, they forecast the emergence of the 'symmetrical family' in which:

> society will have moved from (a) one demanding job for the wife
> (i.e. in the home) and one for the husband (i.e. in paid work)
> through (b) two demanding jobs for the wife and one for the
> husband, to (c) two demanding jobs for the wife and two for the
> husband. The symmetry will be complete. Instead of two jobs there
> will be four.[3]

Twenty years later, the inequalities between women and men are still more noticeable than any new symmetry. In 1985, the average British woman spent 3½ hours a day in housework and childcare: the average British man spent less than one hour.[4] But the picture is changing. As I explain later in this chapter, women in Britain and most other industrial countries are doing less housework than they did thirty years ago and men are doing more. At the same time, both mothers and fathers are spending more time with their children.

As women stay in the labour market for a growing proportion of their working lives, the rigid division of work between women and men is disappearing. One effect is to put considerable pressure on the 'time budgets' of working families. The housework, shopping and other family responsibilities which the woman previously did during the weekday, now have to be fitted into evenings and weekends by the woman alone, or shared by both partners – or done by other people. This pressure on time is, of course, even greater for single parents with paid employment than for two-earner couples.

There are two ways of looking at the division of domestic work: first, to ask people who is *responsible* for different tasks in the household; and second, to measure the *time* spent by women and men in different tasks. Before looking in detail at how much time is spent working in the home, I review the survey evidence about how much women and men share domestic responsibilities.

Who is responsible for domestic work?

When couples are asked who is responsible for domestic work, the answer is overwhelmingly the woman. For instance, the 1980 Women and Employment Survey found that only one in four couples shared the housework equally. The British Social Attitudes (BSA) surveys throughout the 1980s also found that, in four out of five couples, the woman was mainly responsible for 'general domestic duties.'[5]

But these average figures hide the big difference which is made by women's employment. Women employed full-time get the most help from their partners. Women without employment get the least – and women working part-time get only a little more.

For instance, the 1980 survey found that where the wife worked full-time, nearly half the couples said that they shared housework equally. In couples where the woman worked part-time, only one-quarter shared housework equally; where the woman had no employment, fewer than one in five shared it.[6] A study carried out by the advertising agency Lowe Howard-Spink in 1991, which cheerfully proclaimed the 'death of the housewife', showed women employed full-time getting nearly three times as much extra household help from their partners as women employed part-time.[7]

The BSA survey in 1987 also found that women working part-time carried virtually the same responsibility for house and family as women who were not employed. Over 90% of both groups did all the washing and ironing, and nearly as many made all evening meals and did all the household cleaning.[8]

Even amongst couples who are both working full-time, the inequalities are striking. In the 1980 survey, over half of these women did most or all of the housework, compared with only one in fifty of the men. More depressing still, the 1987 BSA survey found that over two-thirds of the women with full-time jobs were solely responsible for general domestic duties; nearly two-thirds of them made the meal every evening, and four out of five did all the washing and ironing. The only household task which was overwhelmingly done by men was repairing household equipment.[9]

In the mid-1980s, Julia Brannen and Peter Moss of the Thomas Coram Research Unit conducted a detailed study of some 60 couples who both worked full-time and who had recently had a child. They also found that the women, on average, did well over half the domestic work. Although over half the husbands routinely did the shopping and half regularly cleared away meals, one in five never prepared a main meal and two-thirds never washed or ironed clothes. Similarly, the study found that these full-time employed women spent an average of 25 hours a week in sole charge of their child compared with only 6 hours for the fathers.[10]

But not all the news is bad. The 1980 survey found that two-thirds of the women in couples where the woman worked full-time *or* part-time reported that she shared childcare 'half and half' with her partner. (A slightly higher proportion of the men reported equal sharing of childcare!) Perhaps surprisingly, around a third of couples where the woman had no other job also reported that they shared the childcare. Interestingly, a majority of women and men in all groups felt that the husband did 'about the right' amount of childcare.

It is important to remember that employed mothers rely more on their partners to look after the children than on any other form of childcare. Half of the mothers in the 1980 survey – including nearly two-thirds of part-timers with school-age children and nine out of ten part-timers working evenings or nights – left the children with their partner while they were at work.[11] One in five of the fathers in the Brannen and Moss survey had sole charge of the child for at least part of the time when the mother was at work. And the BSA survey in 1990 confirmed that over half of employed women with a child under twelve years old relied on partner or grandmother for childcare.[12]

The 1987 BSA survey also found that two in five of the couples working full-time shared the care of sick children; half of them shared the shopping, a third shared the household cleaning and a quarter shared preparing the evening meal.[13] In the Brannan and Moss survey, almost all the men regularly played with their child; nearly half shared night-time duties, changed nappies and fed the child most or every day, although only a third regularly bathed or dressed the child.

Family shifts

Further evidence about the relationship between work and family comes from three related studies carried out in Northampton by members of the Department of Applied Economics at Cambridge University.[14] As one would expect, most couples worked hours that overlapped with each other. But parents of young children who both worked were more likely to have 'staggered' starting and finishing times, with one parent leaving home later than the other and/or returning home earlier. Although this 'family shift system' was more likely to reinforce the woman's domestic responsibilities – she went to work later and/or returned home earlier – the authors conclude that 'there was evidence of a sizeable minority of men in families with children who arrived home significantly before their female partners and thus could be expected to be involved in assuming some domestic responsibilities.'

In the same survey, a quarter of the fathers helped look after their children during school holidays; one-third cared for them after school where their partners worked part-time and one in five did so where their partners worked full-time – again suggesting that a 'family shift system' is more likely when the woman works part-time, particularly including evening hours.

Changing for the better

Although the inequalities remain, changes are happening – and the change is in the right direction.

Detailed analysis of time use surveys (see below, p.56) reveals that, compared with the early 1960s, men are doing a lot more domestic work. The proportion of men with full-time jobs who cook, wash up, shop or do general housework more than doubled between 1961 and 1985. There are still fewer men involved in all these activities than women, but the gap is closing.

Although it is still widely believed that men's domestic work is very different from women's – men do the DIY and gardening, women the cooking, cleaning and washing – the time use surveys also show a marked increase in the proportion of women involved in repairs and other 'odd jobs'. By 1985, women with part-time jobs or not employed were just as likely as men to do household repairs and maintenance (over four out of five of all three groups) and women with full-time jobs were not far behind.

The British Social Attitudes surveys have repeatedly found that people are far more likely to believe that couples living together *should* share household duties and childcare than actually do so in practice. But belief in the ideal of sharing has grown quite markedly during the 1980s, particularly amongst younger people. Combined with the move of younger, better-educated women up the occupational ladder, there is reason to believe that the gap between women's and men's domestic work will continue – slowly – to decline.

Time use surveys from other countries show similar trends. In Norway, for instance, with one of the highest proportions of women in the labour market in Europe and Scandinavia, women still carry the main burden of housework. But fewer women are carrying the burden *alone*. Amongst women aged 25 to 44 living in households with more than one adult, the proportion who were solely responsible for the housework fell from 45% in 1980 to 32% in 1987.[15]

How much time do we spend on housework?

Men are becoming more involved in childcare and housework. But how much *time* do women and men spend on these activities?

More detailed evidence is available for Britain and most other industrial countries from the 'time use' surveys carried out by the BBC and several commercial companies. These date back at least over the last two to three decades; indeed, there are some dating from the last century. Time use surveys use daily diaries and/or detailed, structured interviews to record respondents' activities under several given headings – including paid work and travel to work; routine housework; childcare; shopping and travel to the shops; and leisure.

Time use surveys not only provide a snapshot of how much time women and men spend in domestic work in a particular week, and how this varies according to employment status. They also provide a picture of how time use is changing over several decades. These general trends are of greater interest, and likely to be more reliable, than the precise figures at any one time. The material about time use surveys which follows is drawn almost entirely from Jonathan Gershuny's pioneering collection and analysis of time use surveys from the UK, USA, Canada, Denmark, Norway and the Netherlands between the early 1960s and the mid-1980s.[16] The three British surveys took place in 1961, 1974/5 and 1983/4.

If routine housework and childcare are considered together, then the average British adult of working age is spending much the same amount of time on domestic work as in the early 1960s – about two hours a day. But the average conceals striking changes between different kinds of work – housework, shopping/domestic travel and childcare – and between men and women.

Six hours less for women, three hours more for men

Between 1961 and 1985, the time spent by the average British woman of working age on routine housework – cooking, cleaning, washing clothes and so on – fell by 55 minutes a day or about 6½ hours a week. Since men's daily housework also declined by a few minutes between the 1961 and 1975 surveys, it is reasonable to conclude that the changes in women's lives during this earlier period were closely related to the rapidly spreading ownership of domestic appliances. Very similar trends are revealed by the cross-country comparisons.

Since the mid-1970s, however, men of working age have been doing *more* routine housework. As Table 3.1 shows, women still spend four times as long on housework as men (162 minutes a day for women in 1985, compared with 40 minutes for men). But women's housework time is going down while men's is going up. Compared with 1961, the time men spend on housework has more than doubled.

Unlike the decrease in women's housework, the increase in men's housework time took place entirely between the 1970s and the 1980s. It probably therefore reflects ideological changes as well as the practical pressures associated with married women's move into paid employment.

Paid work affects housework in different ways for men and women. As women increase the time they spend in paid employment, they do not shed an equivalent amount of domestic work. Roughly, for every extra hour of paid work, women do half-an-hour less domestic work. As the *total* amount of time spent on housework has fallen, all women,

Table 3.1 Time spent on routine housework (minutes per average day spent in routine domestic work by men and women aged 20–60, UK)

	Minutes per average day		
	1961	1975	1985
Men			
All	17	15	40
Full-time employed	11	13	35
Part-time employed	40	25	49
Un- or non-employed	61	42	64
Women			
All	217	193	162
Full-time employed	111	112	102
Part-time employed	248	200	188
Un- or non-employed	295	245	198

Source: Gershuny

whatever their work status, have benefitted. But the biggest gains have been for women without employment, the smallest for those working full-time. The less time women spend in paid employment, the more time they spend in housework; but the more time spent in housework, the greater the reduction in housework time.

For women aged between 25 and 44, who are most likely to have young children, the trends are particularly clear. In 1961, full-time housewives averaged nearly 340 minutes' housework, over 5½ hours, a day. By the 1980s, that had dropped to about 250 minutes or just over 4 hours a day. For the woman employed for 40 hours a week, housework dropped from about 190 minutes or about 3 hours a day in 1961 to about 125 minutes, or about 2 hours a day.[17]

Like women, men working full-time do less housework than those who are unemployed or working part-time. But when we look at the *changes* that have taken place since the 1960s, the pattern for men is the reverse of women. Unemployed men are doing the same amount of housework as they were in 1961: but men with full-time jobs are doing nearly half an hour a day more housework, or nearly 3 hours a week.

Nonetheless, the latest BBC survey, carried out in 1989, confirms the very long hours which some women put in to housework. Nearly one in ten women with part-time jobs and about one in twenty women with full-time jobs or who are not employed report doing housework at 7 a.m., compared with only a handful of employed men. At 10 p.m., 1 in 20 of all women are still doing housework, compared with a negligible

1% of employed men. For some women at least, it remains true that a woman's work is never done.

Shopping takes more time

Unlike routine housework, the time we spend shopping and travelling to shops has *increased* dramatically since the early 1960s – from around 40 to around 70 minutes each day, or an increase of 3½ hours a week. As Gershuny observes, 'the service that was once provided by the shopkeeper in the neighbourhood shop, of selection of goods from the shelves, packing the order and conveying it to the point of sale, is now provided by the shopper him or herself. . . . The larger the supermarket, the more walking for the shopper and the greater the average distance from the shopper's home (hence, the longer the travel time). The retail industry, in effect, *externalises* a large part of its costs; retail prices fall and presumably profits rise – and what were financial costs to the producer are translated into time costs for the consumer.'[18] The external costs of this process are also the environmental costs of more and longer car journeys.

At the same time, shopping is an increasingly popular leisure activity for both women and men: it cannot all be classified as domestic work.

As we saw earlier, the proportion of men involved in domestic shopping has increased markedly since the 1960s. Partly as a result, the average man with a full-time job now spends nearly half an hour a day shopping – close to the 37 minutes spent shopping daily by women with full-time jobs. But it is women with part-time or no employment who have experienced the greatest increase in their domestic shopping time, to over an hour a day by 1985.

Children: Seven hours a day, seven days a week

Looking after children takes more time than most full-time jobs.

In 1984, David Piachaud carried out a study of 55 mothers in York with at least one child aged under five. He concentrated on basic tasks (getting the child up and dressed, feeding, washing, bathing, changing nappies and so on) and on the *extra* time involved in shopping, cooking, washing and cleaning which could be attributed to children. The survey did not try to estimate the time spent on education, play and entertainment; nor did it include being 'on call' to children throughout the night. Two-fifths of the mothers also had paid jobs, mostly part-time.[19]

Piachaud found that, on this basic definition, childcare averaged seven hours a day, seven days a week. Where the youngest child was under two, the average was eight hours daily; it fell to six hours daily where the youngest child was aged two to four.

A full-time mother with a very young child can thus expect a working week of over 50 hours, not counting the housework involved in caring for herself and her partner. As we saw earlier, only a minority of men have such long working hours.

Not surprisingly, nearly half of these mothers felt that their current workload was 'much more' than it had been in their previous full-time job. Only one-third of all the mothers – mainly those with children over two – had at least one hour in the day completely free of caring for a child. The women who had a job had more free spells and found things less tiring than women who were full-time mothers. Presumably, their work was more varied and they had periods away from their children – including the journey to work which, however brief, may offer a respite between the demands of children and those of the workplace.

Spending more time with our children

Compared with the early 1960s, both fathers and mothers are spending more time with their children.

As Table 3.2 shows, mothers with full-time jobs now spend, on average, about 1½ hours a day more looking after their pre-school children than this group did in 1961. Mothers employed part-time, with pre-school children, devote an extra half an hour a day to childcare. And full-time mothers spend nearly three-quarters of an hour day more with their children.

Some of this striking change, however, turns out to be a statistical illusion. In 1961, virtually no mothers of pre-school children had full-time employment. By 1985, the proportion had quadrupled – although it is still only a minority of mothers with children under five who work full-time. The few mothers working full-time in the early 1960s were rather different from those working full-time by the mid-1980s. The earlier group will have been far more concentrated amongst highly-paid professionals and low-paid women in manual jobs: both categories likely to be working very long hours. Furthermore, because the numbers involved in the 1961 survey were so small, the information about their time use is less reliable than for other groups.

But there have also been real changes. Whatever the precise figures, all three groups of women show a clear increase in the time spent with

Table 3.2 Time spent looking after children (minutes per average day, women and men aged 20–60, UK)

| | Minutes per average day | | |
	1961	1975	1985
Women			
Full-time employed			
pre-school children	19	28	107
school children	9	7	12
Part-time employed			
pre-school children	44	57	73
school children	34	12	22
Non- or un-employed			
pre-school children	95	81	137
school children	31	24	37
Men			
Full-time employed			
pre-school children	11	14	44
school children	3	4	8
Non- or un-employed			
pre-school children	48	37	37
school children	25	4	11

Source: Gershuny
Note: The figures given in this table are for time spent looking after children as the person's main activity. Looking after children while doing other things – cooking a meal, shopping, housework and so on – is not included.

children. Gershuny's international comparisons also reveal similar trends for both men and women over the last two decades.

Although British fathers still spend much less time looking after their children than mothers, they are doing more than they used to. The change, as Table 3.2 illustrates, is particularly striking for men with children under the age of five whose childcare time increased from an average 11 minutes a day in 1961 to 44 minutes a day by the mid 1980s. For obvious reasons, school-age children receive much less time from their parents, but here the gap between men and women is closing rapidly.

Why do parents spend more time with their children? For women, the answer appears to lie in two other changes – the reduced time spent on routine housework and the shorter hours involved in full-time work. Where looking after children coincides with other domestic work, then the time use survey will record only the main activity, such as cleaning or cooking, and not the childcare: as routine housework shrinks, the time spent with children becomes visible and also, potentially, more valuable. Furthermore, as various time use surveys demonstrate, even women with *full-time* jobs start to move from paid work to childcare from lunchtime onwards with some 15% looking after their children by 3.30 in the afternoon.

Shorter working hours (at least until the early 1980s) are also a factor for men. But the main reason for the increased time fathers spend with children is probably the increase in their partners' employment. As we saw earlier, there is evidence of couples beginning to co-ordinate their hours of work, so that the father cares for the children for at least some of the time when the mother is at work.

Most mothers and fathers enjoy childcare. Routine housework, by contrast, is widely disliked. The shift in time use over the last three decades, therefore, suggests that for mothers, a substantial reduction in unpleasurable housework, coupled with some reduction in employees' working hours, has permitted an increase in more enjoyable activities – childcare and leisure (as well as in the mixed activity of shopping). For fathers, the time saved in employment has been absorbed by increases in housework, childcare, shopping and leisure.

Caring for other dependent relatives

Most public debate about work and family focuses on children. But adult relatives may need caring for too. The number of over-80s is expected to increase from 2.2 million in 1991 to nearly 3 million in 2025.[20]. Thus, more and more adults in their 40s, 50s and 60s will find themselves partly or wholly responsible for looking after a parent or parent-in-law.

The 1980 survey found that 13% of the women they interviewed were providing some care for an adult dependant, usually a relative. Similarly, a government survey in 1985 found that 14% of all adults – including a quarter of women aged between 45 and 64 – provided informal care to friends or relatives.[21]

A quarter of the women carers in the 1980 survey gave constant attention; a further 13% gave at least 15 hours a week. Not surprisingly, one-fifth of the women said that their work had been affected. In some cases, caring responsibilities had prevented them working at all. Others had had to restrict their hours of work or the time at which they worked, or had needed to take time off in order to look after their dependant.[22]

Comparing couples

Women's hours of domestic work remain longer than men's, just as men's hours of paid work and travel to work remain longer than women's.

The *total* amount of work – paid and unpaid – is not therefore very different for men and women. The amount they are paid and the opportunities they have for training and promotion are, of course, radically different.

A time use survey carried out for Unilever in 1986 confirmed that couples generally have similar *total* working hours. Where both partners were employed, they both worked for about ten hours a day. Women who were at home full-time worked about one hour less a day than their partners. (This group included women without small children: as we saw earlier, the working day of a full-time mother is at least as long as most men's.) Where both partners were retired, the woman's working day was about two hours longer than his, but both had much shorter working days than other groups.[23]

There is a huge gulf between women's time and men's time. Just as men continue to put in long hours of paid work, women continue to take the main burden of housework and childcare. There are some encouraging signs of men doing more at home. But the greatest signs of change, perhaps not surprisingly, are in families where both partners are working full-time. The domestic workload of women employed part-time is very similar to that of the full-time mother and housewife.

And here is the dilemma. A further extension of part-time and flexible employment for women may do little to improve women's exclusion from the most responsible and rewarding opportunities at work, and even less to challenge men's absenteeism from the home. But the alternative – that women should adopt male working hours and employment patterns – simply does not meet the aspirations of most women. In the next chapter, I look at the attitudes of women and men towards working time.

4 HOW PEOPLE FEEL ABOUT WORKING TIME

When we think about working time issues, most of us start from full-time work as the norm and the ideal. We generally assume that part-time workers are only reluctantly part-time and that most would prefer full-time jobs. Similarly, most people assume that full-time workers want shorter working hours, although in practice they may not be able to afford it. In fact, attitudes amongst employees as a whole – part-timers as well as full-timers – are considerably more complex than we generally recognise.

I have already referred to several working time surveys, which I shall use again in this chapter. Such surveys are invaluable in helping us to understand people's working time preferences. But they cannot always explore the background to respondents' answers. In order to obtain additional information, IPPR commissioned a programme of qualitative research in which groups of eight people, selected from amongst particular age, sex, occupational and family categories, were interviewed in depth about their attitudes towards working time traditions and innovations. By its nature, qualitative research does not provide statistically significant results; it does, however, illuminate the findings of quantitative surveys.

The IPPR discussion groups, who were interviewed during 1990, consisted of:

☐ women with at least one child aged under five, employed part-time or full-time in manual and clerical jobs (such as bank clerk, school dinner lady, town hall clerical worker, manufacturing shift worker) ('C2D' in market research jargon);

☐ women with at least one child of school age, in the same employment categories as the first group;

☐ men aged 25 to 30 without children in junior or middle management jobs in both manufacturing and service companies (BC1);

☐ men in their 50s with grown-up children in middle and senior management jobs in both manufacturing and service companies (BC1);

☐ women with at least one child of pre-school or school age, employed part-time or full-time in professional or managerial (AB) jobs (including a solicitor, biochemist, headteacher and detective);

☐ men with at least one child of pre-school or school age, in professional or managerial (AB) jobs (banker, personnel director, engineer, accountant);

☐ women aged 50 to 70, working part-time or full-time or seeking work (C2D and BC1);

☐ men aged 50 to 70, working part-time or full-time or seeking work (C2D and BC1).

More choice, more control

It is now commonplace to observe that industrialised societies are moving from mass production to more individualised forms of consumption. But the cultural change goes far deeper than the products we buy. The Henley Centre for Forecasting, for instance, argues that 'we will continue to be frustrated at and progressively more successful in rejecting many of those imposed personal structures that have "cramped our (life)styles". This will include rejections of aspects of family life, work, class and, perhaps most interestingly of all, a conception of "reality" as something constant and given'. The consequences, they believe, will include the emergence of 'radically different activity patterns' and the search for 'new, more freely chosen activities . . . to structure our time'.[1]

Henley's own major survey of changing attitudes found that two-thirds of people would 'prefer to choose my own hours rather than have the routine and discipline of regular hours'. Although those in professional jobs were somewhat more likely to want to control their own working time, at least three out of five people in every social group agreed with the statement.

Many people are already involved in working unconventional hours – and many more are interested in doing so. In this chapter, I start by looking at the working time preferences of full-time and part-time employees, and at the differences between men and women and between those with young children and those without. I then look at employees' attitudes towards various forms of non-standard working and towards a variety of working time innovations. Finally, I suggest how different working time preferences reflect different stages of women's and men's life-cycles.

Full-time or part-time?

Obviously, people's working time preferences are substantially constrained by the jobs that are available, by financial needs and by social attitudes and structures. It is, nonetheless, possible to establish how full-timers and part-timers view their present working arrangements and whether they would like, if at all possible, to change them.

The JCF survey found that virtually all – nine out of ten – of its full-time respondents worked full-time 'by choice'. But one in three hoped or expected to work part-time at some stage in the future, a proportion that was significantly higher amongst older people. Nearly half of those aged 45 to 54 and over half of those aged between 55 and 64 said they would like to work part-time in future or expected to do so. IPPR's qualitative research also found real interest in working shorter hours amongst older people. The British Social Attitudes (BSA) survey in 1990 similarly found that about one in three full-time employees – men and women – would prefer to work fewer hours each week.[2]

Amongst part-time respondents to the JCF survey, 85%, or nearly nine out of ten, also said that they worked part-time by choice. They were no more likely than the full-timers to want to change their hours radically: just under one-third said they hoped or expected to work full-time in future. Similarly, over half of the part-timers said that they would not want to work any overtime and fewer than one in ten wanted overtime of more than ten hours a week. In 1991, when high interest rates were putting even greater pressure on people's earnings, the EOC found that one in four part-timers would like to work longer hours for more pay.[3]

The Northampton survey found that only one-fifth of men would ever consider a part-time job, compared with four-fifths of the women. Amongst the women, over half would *only* consider a part-time job; a further quarter would consider working either full-time or part-time and only one-fifth would only consider a full-time job.[4]

The 1980 Women and Employment Survey (with a much larger sample than the JCF survey, of women only) also found that part-time women employees were more satisfied with their working hours than full-time women workers, a result confirmed by the EOC survey in 1991. Three-quarters of women part-time employees in the latter survey found their total working hours 'very convenient', compared with half of women and around one-third of men working full-time.[5] Part-time working women were also more than twice as likely to be 'extremely satisfied' with the time they had for their families *and* for themselves.

It seems, therefore, that around one-third of full-timers would like, at some stage in their lives, to work part-time and that an even higher proportion of full-timers in their 50s would like to do so. A rather lower proportion of part-timers would like to work longer hours, though not necessarily full-time.

What do part-time employees really want?

All the surveys I have referred to found that part-time employees are happier with their working hours and conditions than full-time workers.

The JCF survey found, for instance, that part-time workers were more satisfied than full-time employees with their basic wage, found their job rather more satisfying and interesting and were more likely to find hours at work and hours outside work equally enjoyable.

The Women in Employment Survey similarly found that, even though part-timers had often moved down from higher level jobs, 'they were overall no less likely than women working full time to find work stimulating or worthwhile.' Both full-timers and part-timers said that the most satisfactory aspect of their work was the people they worked with; for part-timers, their working hours and the ease of their journey to work were equally satisfying. For both groups, the opportunity to use their abilities and their prospects were least satisfying – suggesting that the under-utilisation of women's skills is as prevalent in full-time as part-time occupations.[6]

Although the Women in Employment Survey did not obtain comparative data for men, information about both men and women is available in the recent EOC survey. The EOC found that although most people were happy with their present working hours, women were more satisfied than men, and women employed part-time were more satisfied than either women or men working full-time.

According to this survey, women working part-time were particularly happy with the balance between work, family and leisure: two-thirds were 'extremely satisfied' with the time they had available for their family, compared with less than one-third of men and women working full-time. Perhaps more surprisingly, over half the part-time group were equally satisfied with the time they had to themselves, compared with just over one in five of the full-timers. Confirming what we know about the imbalance of domestic work between women and men, the EOC survey found that around one in three of the women working full-time were 'tired or exhausted' after work, compared with only one in five of both male full-timers and women working part-time.[7] Similarly, a Gallup survey in early 1992 commissioned by the retail group, BhS, and the Working Mothers Association, found that the longer the hours worked, the more difficult women found it to combine work and motherhood.[8]

But perhaps part-time employees are more satisfied with their working hours simply because their family responsibilities leave them with little choice. As the authors of the 1980 survey commented: 'In some ways it is not surprising that such a high proportion of part time workers were happy with their hours of work; unless they can find a job with suitable hours they are unlikely to be able to work at all.'[9] The authors of the Northampton survey likewise suggest that 'women who return to or remain in work when children are young only tend to do so when they have jobs which offer them considerable autonomy in determining their own working-time.'[10]

Nurseries for children or time for parents

None of these surveys asked women working part-time whether they would prefer to work full-time if full-time child care were also available. The 1990 BSA survey, however, asked mothers in employment to imagine that they could choose whatever childcare they liked. Even when faced with the possibilities of a workplace nursery, a free council nursery or a childminder at home, over half of these women – and two-thirds of those with school-age children – said that they would prefer to work only while their children were at school. Just as popular, particularly for children aged under five, was having a relative (including the child's father) care for them for at least some of the time while the mother was working.[11] The survey confirmed that there is a demand for nurseries and childminders which is simply not being met at present. But it also revealed that the form of childcare provision which the majority of working mothers would choose is, in fact, more *time* for themselves and their partners to spend with their children.

The same survey also suggested that if nurseries, childminders and other forms of childcare – including husbands and other relatives – were freely available, only a minority of women now working part-time or not employed at all would choose to work full-time. Around one in six women with children under the age of twelve, and now working part-time, say they would prefer to work full-time if they could get the childcare of their choice, with a similar number wanting to increase their part-time hours. Half of those not currently employed would like work, part-time, with only one in eight wanting full-time work. Amongst those already working full-time, a quarter would *reduce* their hours if they could get childcare to match.

We asked women in the IPPR discussion groups about their ideal patterns of work and childcare. None of the women currently working part-time in the non-professional group expressed a wish to work full-time even if child-care were available. As I explain further below (see p.80), these women felt they had considerable flexibility in their lives already. Most of them intended to develop their careers – a term they used themselves – as their children grew older, but they were clear about wanting more time at home when their children were young. Asked about their priorities, these women unanimously chose their children: 'You have to put them first'. The different groups of men saw work as their first priority, although those with children related that to their family responsibility: 'Most of us have a home and family, we have to provide for them.'

Perhaps surprisingly, the IPPR group of women in professional and managerial jobs were much less satisfied with their lives than the lower-paid women. More of them were working full-time; all of them felt under intense pressure as they tried to juggle the demands of children, job, partner and home. Many already had flexible working hours, often informally agreed with their boss and would welcome more flexibility. But part-time work would mean an even greater setback: 'You don't get promoted if you're part-time'. More women are returning to work full-time after having a child (see above, p.12), a pattern that is particularly marked amongst women in higher-status jobs. But the evidence from both opinion surveys and discussion groups suggests that many will find the combination unsatisfactory.

The BhS survey referred to earlier also found that more than nine out of ten employed mothers wanted employers to offer flexible working hours and more part-time jobs. Nearly as many wanted the options of job sharing and longer (for example, school) holidays, unpaid if necessary. All these 'time' options were even more popular than workplace nurseries or other help with childcare. Similarly, a detailed study of mothers seeking employment in Newcastle found that the two largest barriers the women faced were training and time, with jobs in school hours and school terms seen as ideal.[12]

Table 4.1: More time or more money: European attitudes

	Shorter Hours	Better Pay
Denmark	51	38
Netherlands	47	46
Italy	39	55
Belgium	36	58
Luxembourg	36	58
Spain	31	64
West Germany	30	56
France	30	62
Greece	26	68
United Kingdom	19	77
Ireland	19	78
Portugal	11	82

Source: European Community employee survey 1985.86 and Eurobarometer.

The consistent survey findings that part-time employees are more satisfied with their work, their working hours and the rest of their time do not appear, therefore, to be simply a matter of women making the best of a bad job. Working shorter hours when family responsibilities are greatest is, for many women, a positive choice which provides real benefits.

More time or more money?

Several surveys have explored the extent to which people would trade shorter working hours for less pay. A Eurobarometer survey in 1985 and 1986 asked people throughout the European Community whether they would prefer a wage rise or a reduction in working hours in the next pay round. Overall, nearly two-thirds wanted more money rather than more leisure. But as Table 4.1 shows, there are big differences in attitudes between the EC countries.

The JCF survey also asked respondents whether they would prefer to go on working the same hours for higher wages, or to reduce their hours and earn the same wages. In effect, people were asked whether they would prefer to take their next wage rise in money or in time. Over half of the respondents said they would prefer higher wages for the same hours, with around one-third preferring lower hours for the same wages. While three-quarters of the 16–24 year-olds preferred higher wages, half of the over-55s wanted shorter hours. Although women were more likely to prefer shorter hours and men to prefer higher wages, these differences were less striking than those between the youngest and the oldest workers.

The JCF survey went on to ask people whether they would like to increase or to reduce their working hours, *with a corresponding increase or reduction in pay*. Faced with this choice, only one in twenty opted for shorter hours. Half of those interviewed said they would choose the same hours at the same pay; one in three preferred even longer hours and more pay. Again, the over-55s were more likely than other groups to choose shorter hours. Men were much more likely than women to opt for longer hours and higher earnings; women were most likely to choose the same hours at the same pay.

In its 1990 survey, British Social Attitudes found a similar pattern. Although one-third of men in theory would prefer shorter hours, only one in eight of this group would be willing to accept a pay cut in return. Women were three times as likely to choose shorter hours even at the expense of lower earnings.[13]

The EOC survey in 1991 also asked respondents how they would trade money and time, with three options all based on the same hourly wage: shorter hours and less pay, the same hours and same pay, or longer hours and more pay. The results were very similar to the JCF survey, with one-fifth of the men opting for longer hours and more pay. A quarter of the part-time employees said they would choose longer hours with more pay, confirming earlier findings that a minority of part-time workers are!under-employed. Consistent with the BSA survey, nearly one-fifth of the women full-time employees, however, would prefer shorter hours even at the cost of lower pay.[14]

Interestingly, the BhS survey also asked employed mothers how they felt about their *partners'* working hours. Over half said that they would prefer him to work shorter or more flexible hours, so that he could help more with the family and give the woman more time for her own job. The possibility of a drop in the man's income was not, however, referred to.

We explored the idea of working fewer hours for less pay with our discussion groups. Both men and women generally felt that they – or, for many of the women who already worked shorter hours, their husbands – would love to have the chance to work fewer hours while their children were young, but that no-one could afford to do it in practice. Since these discussions took place in 1990, it is hardly surprising that most of the people we talked to were already having trouble keeping up with mortgage payments; any cut in the family income was simply not an option.

As the Eurobarometer survey suggested, one would expect greater interest in shorter hours, even with some loss of pay, in countries like Denmark and West Germany where wage levels and living standards are significantly higher than in Britain. For instance, a survey in Sweden by the Ministry of Labour in the early 1980s produced very different results from the British surveys. In that survey, over half of full-time employees said they would prefer shorter working hours with the same pay to higher wages for the same hours. When asked whether they would prefer to increase working hours and income, or to reduce both, nearly one in five Swedish employees opted for shorter working hours, with only one in ten wanting to increase their hours and income.

Shorter working day, shorter working year, shorter working life?

Shorter working hours can come in many different forms. Half an hour off the working day could become 2½ hours off a full-time week or half a day off a fortnight. It could become an extra three weeks' holiday a year or, more dramatically, over two years' earlier retirement.

Several surveys have explored people's attitudes towards these and other working time innovations. We also considered the issue in some detail in the IPPR groups. The consistent and striking conclusion is that most people prefer longer blocks of time off to a shorter working day.

The JCF survey asked respondents *how* they would prefer to take a reduction in working hours: shorter hours each week; the same hours each week, with longer holidays; or the same hours each week, with earlier retirement. Although the trade union movement has traditionally emphasised a shorter working day and week, the most popular option – preferred by nearly four in ten people – was longer holidays. Three in ten preferred earlier retirement with only two in ten choosing the shorter working week.

Not surprisingly, attitudes differed between women and men as well as between different age groups. Men were most likely to prefer earlier retirement with longer holidays the next most popular choice. In contrast, nearly half the women preferred longer holidays, with a shorter working week coming second and earlier retirement third. Not surprisingly, earlier retirement was the most popular choice amongst older workers (over one-third of all those aged 55 to 64); longer holidays were most popular amongst the young (over half of 16 to 24-year-olds).

The JCF survey asked a further question which offered a bigger range of options: a five-day working week with fewer hours each day; a four-day working week with more hours each day; an unchanged working week and longer holidays; earlier retirement; sabbatical leave; and a longer period of education/training before starting work. Again, longer holidays were popular, preferred by about three people in ten. But faced with this menu of options, more people preferred the four-day working week – even at the expense of a longer working day – with full-time employees, especially men, keenest of all. Longer holidays in return for an unchanged working week were preferred by part-time employees and by women. The shorter working day – often regarded as the most desirable working pattern, particularly for parents with young children – was chosen by fewer than one in five of the women.

Earlier retirement was, again, more likely to be favoured by older workers, but it is interesting that nearly twice as many amongst this age-group preferred an unchanged working week with longer holidays – suggesting perhaps that they wanted to phase in retirement gradually, rather than opting for earlier, full-time retirement.[15]

By contrast, the EOC survey in 1991 found a high level of satisfaction with present working time arrangements: nearly two-thirds of the people they surveyed could not think of any way in which they would want to change their hours. Around one in ten of men and women working full-time would prefer to start and finish work earlier and a further one in ten of full-time employed women wanted more flexibility.[16] The PSI survey on maternity leave also found that one-fifth of new mothers wanted more flexible working arrangements.[17]

Again, Scandinavian surveys reveal a different pattern of preferences. In Sweden, for instance, the shorter working day – particularly for women – and longer holidays – particularly for men – are the preferred options, followed by earlier retirement. The shorter working day – which has statutory support – is also particularly popular with parents of pre-school age children.[18]

An extensive survey carried out in Norway for the Commission on Working Time Reform found that, amongst the workforce as a whole, the shorter working day or week was much less popular than allowing early retirement for those who wanted it. (In Norway, the retirement age is 67 for both women and men.) When respondents were asked how they would prefer to take a reduction of five hours in the working week, longer holidays were overwhelmingly the most popular choice except amongst women with children below school age, nearly half of whom preferred a shorter working day. Amongst women with school-age children, longer holidays were again more popular than a shorter working day.[19] Similar support for longer blocks of leisure time, rather than small reductions in the working day, has been reported in a number of German surveys.[20]

Talking about time

In the IPPR discussion groups, there was considerable interest in the idea of giving people as much choice as possible about how working hours were distributed. There were, however, substantial differences between the non-professional and the professional groups, as well as between women and men.

In all the groups, flexitime was universally welcomed. Many of the women also strongly favoured a four-day week, even at the expense of longer daily working hours. Similarly, they liked the idea of trading off a longer working day against longer holidays, particularly if those could fit in with school holidays.

The mothers we interviewed in manual and other non-professional jobs all wanted term-time working. They were more than willing to trade term-time working for longer days, or indeed to work full-time during school terms, preferring this arrangement to 'part-time' (that is, year-round part-time) work. The shorter working day – which many of the women, as part-timers, already worked – was a less popular option. The professional groups, however, saw term-time employment as only appropriate to lower-grade jobs.

The men in our discussion groups were more interested in how staggered working patterns would reduce traffic congestion, but tended to be conservative about the possibility for flexibility in their own firms or industries. Presumably because the men we interviewed were mostly working a standard five-day week, often with long daily hours, they seemed unaware of the extent to which more flexible working arrangements already exist in many enterprises.

Many of the men to whom we talked could not imagine exchanging longer working days for longer holidays since this would reduce their companies' competitiveness. As one of the respondents commented: 'We all work long days – we must have months of holiday owing'. For these men, the pressures at work were already so great that there seemed little hope of reorganising their working time. When a specific example was given – of a young, childless man choosing to work six days a week in return for 12 weeks' holiday a year – the older men, again, thought that no company could operate like this and that anyone who could be spared for so long wasn't really needed. The younger men, however, were extremely enthusiastic: 'Where can I sign up?' was a typical response.

The men's reactions to the idea of term-time working were also mixed. The older men generally felt it was a preposterous idea – obviously unaware that companies like Boots and IBM have pioneered it successfully. As one respondent said: 'It's not an ideal world – it just wouldn't work'. When the group was offered a particular example, of a mother of three working during term-time, the general reaction was that she would have to work in education. There was, however, some recognition that companies would have to adapt to the needs of working mothers. The group of younger men to whom we talked generally approved of term-time working – for their future wives!

When the idea of flexible working hours was translated into the example of a man in his 50s who wanted to put off retirement and continue working for as long as he could, but who had cut down to three days a week to have more time working on his house, the older men suddenly became enthusiastic about flexible working: 'That would be perfect, I'd love to be able to do that'; 'I'm doing up our house at the moment – if I'd had the chance to cut down to three days a week, I'd have taken it.' Many of the older men seemed to be taking a growing interest in their families than they had done when their children were young: 'I spend more time with my grandchildren than I did with my kids at the same age.' Shorter hours for older workers were also supported by the groups of women and younger men to whom we talked.

How people feel about overtime

As we have seen, a large number of men working full-time would be willing to work even longer hours for more money. The EOC survey, which found one in five men making this choice, commented that: 'The demand for extra hours by the full-time men who were already working such long hours is very depressing. That they were prepared to trade even more of their limited time for more money suggests a very real constraint on the ability of the trade union movement to get very far with effecting their aim of reducing real working hours.'[21]

The JCF survey also found that one in three people wanted to work longer hours for more pay, rather than the same hours, or shorter hours for less pay. Of those who preferred longer hours, however, nearly half only wanted between one and five hours overtime a week; only one-fifth wanted over ten hours a week. Of the total sample, therefore, less than one in ten wanted overtime in excess of 10 hours a week. As Rathkey points out: 'This at a time when the *average* overtime per overtime worker in manufacturing industry is very close to 10 hours a week.'[22] Overall, two-thirds of the JCF survey wanted either no overtime or no more than five hours a week.

Not surprisingly, as the Northampton survey found, women are much less willing to work regular overtime than men. Although the hours of women in full-time jobs are shorter on average than those of men, the EOC survey found that only one in ten of women full-timers would be prepared to trade longer hours for more pay.

Night and weekend work

The Northampton survey found that amongst both men and women working nights was the most unpopular working time arrangement. Women's second most unpopular choice was working weekends; for men, it was working evenings. Men without dependent children were just as likely not to want work nights or evenings; fathers with school-age children were the most likely to have problems working weekends, nights and evenings. Almost all the women with children aged under five said they would find it difficult to work weekends or nights, compared with only half of those with school-age children. The age of the children, however, made little difference to women's attitudes to working evenings: less than half said that this would be difficult.[23]

The EOC survey also found that night and weekend work were more unpopular with women than men. Eight out of ten women would find it impossible or extremely inconvenient to work after 11 p.m. or overnight, compared with about half the men. Nearly half the women would object to working after 6 p.m., compared with less than one in five men. Nonetheless, just as there are women as well as men who already work evenings, nights and/or weekends, there are significant minorities of women – as well as larger groups of men – who find non-standard working hours positively convenient.[24]

The IPPR discussion groups confirmed this point. The mothers in non-professional jobs whom we interviewed all placed great importance on fitting their work around their children. Thus, many were willing to consider working not only evenings but also weekends: 'I'd like to have the opportunity to work some weekends'; 'When you've got kids, the more flexible you can be the better.'

Sunday trading and Sunday working

A series of opinion polls since 1981 have found that around two-thirds of the public support changing the Sunday trading laws to permit more shops to open. At the same time, most people do not want Sunday to become just another weekday. For instance, a Harris survey in January 1989 found that two-thirds of respondents preferred Sundays to be a different and more peaceful sort of day. Perhaps surprisingly, however, only 54% in the same survey agreed that Sunday would be spoiled 'if most of the shops were open and it was as noisy and busy as any other day', compared with 42% who disagreed.[25]

More detailed questions about which shops should be open on Sunday produce conflicting answers. The same Harris survey, commissioned by the Keep Sunday Special campaign, found that 88% of people would be satisfied if Sunday trading were confined to essential outlets such as chemists, newsagents and small general food stores. A 1989 MORI survey for the National Consumer Council asked respondents to choose between that proposal and an alternative which would allow all shops to open on Sunday afternoons and small shops only to open on Sunday mornings. This time, 59% preferred the more liberal option and only 32% the narrower proposal.[26]

Sunday shoppers, however, may not want to be Sunday workers. The EOC survey found that over half the women, but only a third of the men, would find it impossible or extremely inconvenient to work on Sundays. Sunday working falls between night shifts and Saturday work on an unpopularity scale. Two-thirds of all employees object to night work, about four in ten object to Sunday working and one-quarter object to Saturday working. Saturday, Sunday and night work are all more unpopular with women than men, and more unpopular with women working part-time than those working full-time. But a significant minority of men and women also say that they would find Sunday working convenient.

Amongst those already working Sundays, the women seem to be rather more content than the men. One in five of the men in the EOC survey worked regular or occasional Sundays: about a quarter of them would prefer not to. Of the 15% of women full-time employees working Sundays, only one in seven would prefer not to; of the 9% of women part-time employees working Sundays, rather less than one in four would prefer not to.[27]

In Germany, Sunday working appears to be much less acceptable. Over two-thirds of those now working on Saturdays and Sundays would prefer to work less often or never on these days.[28]

The IPPR discussion groups generally felt that the present Sunday trading laws were 'ridiculous' and that individuals should be able to choose whether or not to work on Sundays. Although Sunday was no longer a religious festival for the groups, most people felt that it was an important family day. The idea of 'family shifts' – with one partner working, say, three days including a weekend, and the other working during the week – was generally unpopular. But most people welcomed the availability of services on a Sunday: 'If no-one worked on a Sunday what would we do?' They would not be happy, however, to see Sunday becoming a working day like any other: 'It's fine as it is – shouldn't be more widespread.'

Attitudes to parental leave

Maternity leave is popular with mothers. As the PSI survey showed, British women are more than twice as likely today to return to the same employer after having a baby as they were a decade ago. One in four women with small children want improved maternity rights, to make it easier to combine employment with motherhood.[29]

The IPPR discussion groups again showed a striking difference in the attitudes of women and of men. Maternity leave was universally popular with these working mothers, many of whom regretted that they had not worked for long enough or worked too few hours to have qualified themselves. Their expectations of maternity leave were, however, modest: a typical suggestion was that women should be able to choose how long they stayed away, from six weeks to about three months. For the women in professional jobs whom we interviewed, maternity leave was also a subject of considerable agonising over how much time to take off. In contrast, parental leave in Sweden, which can be shared between both parents, is being extended to eighteen months.

The men we interviewed, although willing to acknowledge the importance of maternity leave in principle, were largely uninterested in practice. The older men, particularly the managers, regarded it as 'a nuisance, but a necessity'. And the group of older women, whose children (if any) had grown up, were hostile to the idea of a 'privilege' which their generation had managed without.

The working mothers were also strongly in favour of paternity leave and generally felt that it should be a legal right. They objected to the fact that their husbands had to take days from their annual holiday leave in order to be available when a child was born. They were clear about the purpose of paternity leave; a typical comment was: 'You need them at home – not just for yourself, but to give your other children some reassurance'.

The older men, on the other hand, were appalled at the idea. They clearly felt that, at the time their children were born, their careers were far too important to be interrupted by paternity leave. 'No way,' was the unanimous response, 'I just couldn't have afforded the time.' The younger men, not yet fathers themselves, were much less hostile but seemed rather puzzled by why they might need it: 'I expect it's so you can help out with the shopping and things.'

Women's time, men's time

As the survey evidence makes clear, women and men have very different attitudes to working time – a difference which directly reflects women's double responsibility in the home as well as in the workplace.

We explored these differences further in the IPPR discussion groups, initially by asking the members of each group to describe their daily routine. The women offered extremely detailed routines, starting early in the morning with breakfast for the family, packing school lunches, getting the children dressed and so on, and ending late at night as they did the ironing and other housework. Childcare arrangements were mainly informal, as they are for the majority of working women, and took up a lot of their time. Although employment was important to all the women, very few offered any detail about the actual routines in their job.

In contrast, the men's routines entirely revolved around their work. The day began when they arrived at their place of work; they described a routine of phone calls, meetings, clients and other pressures, and rarely mentioned their homes. The younger men we spoke to did not yet have children; going to the pub and watching TV were their main relaxations. The older men's children were grown up and it is not, therefore, surprising that families did not figure in the daily routine. Other qualitative research, however, suggests that even for fathers of young children, it is work rather than home that structures the daily routine.

The lives of working mothers are already extremely flexible. Most have worked full-time for several years before having their first child; a period of several months or years spent caring for a small child or children is often followed by part-time work; for a growing proportion, there is a period of part-time or full-time employment *between* the birth of the children, as well as a return to long-term employment at some stage after the last child was born. Not suprisingly, therefore, women are generally more familiar with the idea of flexible working time, more open to working time innovations and more willing to support them.

The women we interviewed were all aware of public debate about the 'demographic time-bomb' and its implications for older women workers. They were also clear that re-organising working time could work to everyone's benefit. As individuals, most of them had chosen jobs with hours which suited their families – either officially (for instance, as job-sharers), or through informal arrangements with their managers. As employees, they felt that companies which adapted to their working time needs would be more productive since the workforce would be happier and there would be less absenteeism. 'It works to everyone's benefit – they get more out of you,' was a typical comment.

Many of the women without professional qualifications wanted further training in the future, even though they did not have the time for it while their children were young. Some anticipated a complete change of career when their children were older. The women who already had more senior posts, however, felt that they were paying a price in promotion prospects, even when they were working full-time, by not being able to put in 'that extra ten per cent'. They found it harder to envisage working time changes – other than flexitime – which would enable them to combine high-level careers with their families.

The older women were more dissatisfied with their lives: their children had grown up and needed them less, but their work did not compensate. They found it hard not only to get the hours they wanted ('Often they want you to do the times no-one else wants.') but also the responsibility which they deserved ('I think we're real workers, and more reliable than youngsters, but they don't see it.'). Feeling generally unwanted and undervalued, they were the group who wanted to work most but expected least from the employer.

The group of older men were even more cautious about working time changes and, indeed, seemed unaware of the extent to which working time regimes are already being transformed. Flexitime, for instance, was seen as a 'hassle' for managers, something 'for the women', something that 'we'll have to get used to' rather than a positive benefit. Term-time working, job-sharing, individually determined working hours, paternity leave and similar arrangements were seen as simply impractical. Unlike

Table 4.2: Working time reforms and people's life-cycles

Life phase	Group	Working time issues
Young, independent	Men and women	Longer holidays (possibly paid for by longer days/weeks) More time for education and training Longer hours for more money and promotion
Parental Phase:		
Pre-school children	Women	Maternity, paternity and parental leave More flexible hours Career breaks
	Men	Paternity and parental leave More flexible hours Option to work shorter hours
School-age children	Women	Term-time working/longer holidays (even at expense of longer days/weeks) Time for education and training/retraining Working hours that fit with partner's Option to move into full-time employment
	Men	Four-day week/longer weekends Opportunity to work longer hours for more pay
Older, independent phase	Women and men	Time for education and training/retraining; sabbatical leave Four-day week/longer weekends Longer holidays
Older, caring phase	Women	Option to reduce working hours
Pre-retirement	Women and men	Option to work shorter week/part-time Longer holidays
Retirement	Women and men	Flexible retirement (individual choice of retirement date; option of part-time retirement) Earlier retirement by choice, not compulsion

the women, these men generally felt that working time changes could only operate in a few companies and that they would be disastrous for productivity.

Younger men, however, were more likely to see working time changes as important to themselves as well as economically beneficial. All the groups agreed on the importance of investing more time in training and education. And there was widespread agreement not only that pension ages should be equal for women and men, but also that compulsory retirement should be replaced by flexible retirement.

Attitudes change with people's lifecycles

As one would expect, people's attitudes to working time change are closely linked to the kind of work they do: support for the shorter working week is overwhelmingly to be found amongst full-time male, manual workers. It is also linked to the different phases of women's and men's lives. A single approach to working time change – such as proposals for a shorter working day – cannot reflect the different priorities which women and men have at different stages of their lives.

A trade union study in Norway analysed the link between different working time reforms and different life-cycle phases for women and for men.[30] Table 4.2 applies the same idea to Britain. It is *not* intended to suggest that certain changes are only popular with certain groups – flexible retirement, for instance, is widely supported amongst all age-groups – but illustrates how different changes are directly relevant to different groups. Obviously, the different phases cannot be rigidly separated: families often have both pre-school and school-age children together; and the later stages (caring for a dependent adult, pre-retirement and retirement) are increasingly likely to blur into each other.

Instead of assuming that a single working time pattern is the ideal, policy-makers, managers and trade union negotiators all need to keep in mind the wide variety of people's working time preferences and the relationship between those preferences and the different stages of people's lives.

5 TIME TO CHANGE

As we have seen, the pattern of people's working lives is changing fast. Despite the complexities, some clear trends emerge: shorter hours in paid employment, with a reduction in full-time hours and an increase in part-time work; less time in total housework, with more for men and less for women and some narrowing of the gap between them; more time from both men and women in childcare; and the development of a wide variety of working time contracts which do not fit the full-time standard form.

In the rest of this book, I consider why we should change the organisation of working time in Britain, and how we could do it. In this chapter, I look at the goals of working time reform. Chapter 6 covers the question of state regulation at both British and European level. The two concluding chapters deal with action at the workplace by management and by trades unions.

Goals

There are four general objectives which could be served by working time reform:

First, to safeguard employees and the general public against the health and safety consequences of excessively long or otherwise dangerous working hours. This may appear a minimal requirement: but the link between long hours and health and safety risks is not accepted by the British government or reflected in legislation.

Second, to promote the most productive use of the whole workforce. This embraces the need to make organisations more efficient and more competitive, which, as we have seen, has driven much of the working time change now taking place in industrialised countries. But it also includes the goal of shortening working hours in order to reduce unemployment.

Third, to enable individuals to work hours which give them more choice about how to combine paid employment with family, education, leisure and community activities. This aim – greater working time autonomy – has always been the driving force behind workers' campaigns for *shorter* working hours. Today, as the evidence about people's preferences suggests, it includes the aim of enabling people to *vary* their working hours – and, thus, the balance between employment and other activities – at different times of their lives.

Fourth, to reduce the conflicts between work and family and thus to reduce the inequalities between women and men in paid and unpaid work. As we have seen, there are substantial differences between men's and women's working time and working lifetimes. Changing working time can have an important role to play in strategies for more equal opportunities.

In the rest of this chapter, I use these four objectives as criteria against which to measure the costs and benefits of the kind of changes described earlier in this report. Only by taking a view on the desirability or undesirability of these changes can we decide on appropriate strategies for government, employers and trades unions.

Do long hours damage your health?

Some working time arrangements – such as extremely long hours and night work – have more serious implications for health and safety than others.

Long working hours come in two forms: long hours worked regularly for most or all of the year, often involving night and/or shift work; and long hours worked in return for long blocks of time off. There are costs and benefits in both.

Where long hours are worked regularly – as they are by many men doing manual jobs or working as doctors, managers or other professionals – the costs include the possible effects on employees' health and their own and other people's safety, as well as a possible loss of productivity. Employees may also suffer from the loss of leisure and social life and the disruption of their families.

The Conservative government, however, does not accept that long working hours can be a health hazard. Following the abolition of legislation which restricts the hours of employment for young people, Patrick Nicholls MP, Under Secretary of State for Employment, stated that 'there is no evidence to suggest working long or unsocial hours [presents] risks to health'.[1]

There is in fact substantial evidence from research in several countries about the damaging effect of long working hours and different shift systems, particularly those involving night work or a frequent change between night and day shifts. For instance, a 1976 study of shift workers in three British steel plants concluded that most had suffered sleep disorders, problems with appetite and greater nervous tension.[2] A Swedish study of public transport drivers concluded that shift-workers' health was so poor that fundamental changes to the shift systems were required.[3] And a survey of German train drivers found that they were least vigilant at 3 a.m. and 3 p.m., when body rhythms were slowest, with a 24-hour rest period producing the highest levels of vigilance in the subsequent shift.[4]

More general reports support these specific surveys. For instance, a study of shiftworking commissioned by the French Ministry of Labour and published in January 1979 concluded that:

> Individual workers never adjust completely to changes in working hours, but tolerance varies widely from person to person. Night work is probably the most harmful because it prevents regular sleep at night. Insufficient sleep is certainly the cause of many of the pathological symptoms observed.[5]

And a major study by the Japan Association of Industrial Health, which found that shift workers were much more likely than others to suffer chronic fatigue, digestive disorders, ulcers, respiratory problems and cardiovascular disease, recommended strict controls on shift work.[6]

Several German studies have also established a close relationship between long working-hours and tiredness (particularly where extensive overtime is worked) and an increased accident rate. Night-work, whether permanent or alternating with day-work, also causes more stress than a normal working day and, in the long-term, can cause ill-health.[7] Not surprisingly, the effects of long hours, overtime and night work depend very much on the worker's age, health and social class, as well as their occupation.

Hurting other people

The ill-effects of excessive or stressful working hours can, however, extend well beyond the employees concerned. The official enquiry into the Clapham Junction railway disaster in December 1988, which killed thirty-five people, found that the senior technician responsible for the faulty wiring which caused the accident had been working a seven-day week for the previous thirteen weeks. Nor was this unusual: in the same thirteen weeks, over a quarter of the workforce had worked seven days every week and a further third had worked thirteen days out of fourteen.

The enquiry concluded that the 'uncharacteristic' errors made by the technician were caused by:

> the constant repetition of weekend work in addition to work throughout the week which had blunted his working edge, his freshness and his concentration . . . in the three months before the accident he had had one sole day off in the entire 13 weeks. I find this to be totally unacceptable and to be conducive to the staleness and lack of concentration which has been manifested in the evidence . . . It should not have been countenanced and it was a contributory cause to the accident . . . It was not a question of exhaustion which was the culprit, but rather the mental and emotional blunting and flattening which was produced by protracted periods of working every day of the week without the refreshment of time off with family and friends.[8]

Not surprisingly, the enquiry specifically recommended that British Rail should monitor overtime to ensure that no-one worked 'excessive levels of overtime' and introduce 'scheduled hours' (that is, rostering over seven-day periods with a 'scheduled hours payment' to compensate for the withdrawal of overtime) in order to provide staff to carry out work at weekends.

The excessive hours of junior hospital doctors have been widely publicised in the last few years, as government negotiated with the British Medical Association (BMA). A survey in 1987 and 1988 found that junior doctors averaged 90 hours on duty a week, with actual hours worked between 50 and 69. Doctors in teaching hospitals were on duty for over 100 hours. The longest period of rest at night during the week averaged six hours, but for a quarter of nights it was no longer than 4 hours. Not surprisingly, doctors report that their accuracy in prescribing for patients is adversely affected by tiredness and the BMA has argued strongly that cutting hours would substantially improve patient care.[9]

As with doctors, there is no statutory limit on the hours worked by air traffic controllers, although the Civil Aviation Authority is now considering proposals to limit them to 10 hours a day, with a break after two hours at the radar screen. An independent committee reported to the Authority that 'in the interests of safety it would be unwise for the hours of work of civil air traffic controllers to remain formally and anomalously unregulated.'[10]

Conflicts of interest

Total working time flexibility is indeed envisaged by some employers. For instance, the European Foundation in its survey of working time limitations in the European Community reported that:

> Employers insist on the necessity of the adaptability of the enterprise to the changing demands of the market, on the urgent need to be competitive and to disconnect individual working-time and the working-time of the machines, of capital investment; work any time, day, night, Sundays, weekend, when economically useful and indicated.[11]

Neither employers' economic needs for working time flexibility nor employees' need for working time autonomy or more overtime pay should be allowed to create working time regimes which can have such serious and foreseeable consequences as the British Rail overtime system.

But other forms of anti-social working, such as night work, are less easy to judge. Some institutions, including hospitals, cannot function properly unless people work at night. Others, including some manufacturing companies, would be less competitive if night working were banned. If the evidence about the damaging effects of night work is accepted, then there is clearly a conflict of interest: between the needs of individual employees on the one hand, and the needs of the public (in the case of, say, a hospital) or the enterprise on the other. European trade unions have generally opposed night work in principle, arguing for substantially improved working conditions (including shorter hours) where night work is inevitable.[12]

Long daily or even weekly hours may be offset against long weekends or holidays, creating annual hours equivalent to a 40-hour week or shorter and these arrangements are generally popular with employees. Depending on the nature of the occupation and the shift pattern involved, however, the employee may be working on some occasions an extremely long day – eleven, twelve hours or more. Especially where night work is involved, the same health and safety considerations arise.

Because the demands of different jobs are so varied, universal limits on working hours may not be the most satisfactory way of dealing with health and safety issues. But the pressure for harmonisation of working time restrictions within the European Community will require greater regulation than now exists in Britain. Proposals for a new framework, consistent with European standards, are set out in chapter 6.

Economic costs and benefits

Britain's economic problems are severe. The decline in competitiveness within manufacturing industry is reflected in the declining share of domestic and other markets taken by British goods and the growing deficit in manufactured trade. Changes in working time must, therefore, be judged not only by their impact on individual employees, but also by their contribution to economic efficiency.

Shorter working hours and more choice for individual employees may appear at first sight to impose substantial costs on enterprises. The CBI survey of working time revealed managers' fears that 'if not handled carefully, reductions in hours could increase the costs of production and eat their way into profits.'

The CBI quoted a typical comment by a manager in a large conglomerate:

> If anything, reductions in hours without *pro rata* reductions in wages as payment will be met with reductions in employment *not* improvements. When companies are influenced by the profit motive increased costs in one area *must* be met by savings elsewhere. If workers are not prepared to pay for reductions in hours then, as far as I am concerned, those reductions will be resisted.[13]

One-fifth of organisations affected by the basic hours reduction in 1979 were unable in fact to meet the costs of shorter hours through increased productivity.[14]

In both West Germany and Britain, the engineering workers' campaign for a shorter working week was fiercely resisted by employers who warned of disastrous effects on productivity and profits. In most cases, however, their fears were unjustified. In Germany, the agreement to reduce basic hours in the metal industry from 40 to 38½ stipulated that 'on the occasion of fixing new levels of working hours, the working capacity of plant and installations should not be reduced'. Not only did most companies enforce this provision, but some combined the cut in individuals' hours with an extension of plant operating hours.[15]

In Britain, most of the recent agreements for reduced hours – like most of those reached in 1979 – were linked to other changes to increase productivity. Trade union pressure for shorter working hours, particularly in manufacturing industry, has often been met by proposals for extended operating hours, changes in the shift system, rostering of holidays, reduction of meal and tea-breaks, elimination of special payments (e.g., for clocking on and off or for 'washing up time' at the end of shifts) which can more than pay for the costs involved in reducing individuals' working hours. The Institute of Personnel Management's study in 1986 concluded that 'the reduction in the working week has had . . . at worst, only a marginal negative impact on costs.'[16]

There is little doubt that productivity increases can compensate for shorter hours, even to the extent of maintaining previous wage levels, so that unit costs remain the same. As the competitive pressures on British enterprises intensify, however, standing still is not enough. But working time changes may be able to do even more.

Economic incentives for flexibility

The economic importance of flexible working time is the part it plays in strategies for restructuring enterprises to make them more competitive. More flexible working hours and shorter working hours – in a wide variety of forms, including part-time working – can help to achieve productivity gains substantial enough to *reduce* unit costs.

That is why, despite the resistance of engineering employers to the shorter working week, managers have often initiated the reorganisation of working time. In Britain and other European countries, working time flexibility has to a very large extent been driven by economic imperatives. The examples given in chapter 2 illustrate how decoupling individual working hours from the company's operating time enables production to be reorganised to meet consumer demand and/or increase the return on capital equipment.

The Confederation of German Employers' Associations has spelt out the advantages to enterprises of an increase in part-time working, many of which apply to other forms of working time flexibility. They see the main advantages as:

☐ flexible adjustment to changes in demand and satisfactory means of responding to peaks in activity in terms of cost;
☐ improved capacity use through appropriate extension of production time by means of part-time work;
☐ compensation by part-time work of work lost due to reduction of working time [i.e. for full-timers] through collective agreements;
☐ maintenance of longer operating hours and increased availability of services through part-time shifts (commerce, catering);
☐ smooth coverages of vacations and absences;
☐ avoidance or reduction of costly overtime;
☐ reduction of time lost due to production bottlenecks;
☐ greater work satisfaction and motivation;
☐ lower absenteeism and labour turnover;
☐ higher labour productivity;

☐ continued employment of efficient workers who cannot continue on a full-time basis because of family, age or other reasons;
☐ possibility to obtain qualified personnel;
☐ avoidance of dismissals [including redundancy] through change of full-time to part-time work;
☐ possibility to take over qualified personnel in case of lack of full-time jobs;
☐ easier transition to retirement.[17]

As this indicates, working time changes may be a response to a shortage of employees with the right skills. In Britain, before the 1991 recession, labour market pressures, particularly in the south-east, encouraged employers to use flexible working time arrangements to attract into employment more women with children, older people and students. Where employers are having trouble filling vacancies, then potential and actual employees will have more power to determine working time arrangements. But depending on the nature of the enterprise, highly flexible working time patterns, including individual determination of working hours, may also substantially benefit the enterprise.

Do shorter hours mean more jobs?

Reducing unemployment is a central theme in the European trade union movement's concern with working time and one of the most important motives for the West German trade union campaign for a 35-hour week.

Employers and trades unions disagree, however, about the extent to which shortening working hours can create new jobs. The CBI survey referred to earlier, suggested that most managers were extremely sceptical.

In many cases, managers stressed their belief that marginal reductions in hours would not lead to an increased demand for labour unless there were compensating reductions in pay. And if reductions were accompanied by improvements in productivity, not even then. Indeed, there was a general feeling that, if there were not a compensating moderation of pay, reductions in hours if anything would be detrimental to employment. Firms would respond to increased costs by reducing their workforce.[18]

In Germany, too, employers believed that a shorter working week would not create jobs and might even, by increasing costs, lead to higher unemployment. Now that a normal working week of below 40 hours has been negotiated for over 80% of German full-time employees, there is enough data available to assess the employment effects of cutting working hours.

Extensive research carried out by employers' organisations as well as by the trades unions and independent bodies suggests that the reduction of working hours achieved by the German engineering and other unions has indeed kept unemployment significantly lower than it would otherwise have been. A study by the engineering employers' association, Gesamtmetall, found that 24,000 additional jobs had been created as a result of reducing the working week from 40 to 38½ hours in 5,000 of its member companies. A similar study by the union, I.G. Metall, estimated that 102,000 new jobs had been created in the same number of companies.

The German economist, Hartmut Seifert, comments on the results of these and several other studies: 'It is incontrovertible that the agreed shortening of the working week has had a positive effect on developments in employment. Even Gesamtmetall, which originally maintained that there would be an opposite effect, has now shown in two of its own investigations that a positive effect on employment can be detected.' He suggests that, overall, reductions in working time could have increased the number of full-time jobs by between 200,000 and 280,000, together with a further 57,000 – 76,000 part-time jobs. The figures, although impressive, are nonetheless modest compared with an unemployment level between 2.2 and 2.3 million; without working time changes, however, unemployment would have been even higher, at around 2.5 million.[19]

The British experience

In Britain, however, results have been disappointing. The TUC Campaign for Reduced Working Time consistently notes that – despite TUC resolutions calling for a shorter working week, cuts in overtime and the creation of new jobs – record overtime levels in the 1980s threatened the gains made through shorter working hours.[20]

Furthermore, the landmark agreements on shorter working hours in many industrial companies have generally been achieved through a reorganisation of working hours which has delivered substantial productivity gains. Wage levels have been maintained or even increased, despite the reduction in individual working hours; costs have been cut, despite the increases in the hourly wage; job creation, although an element in some agreements, does not appear to have been widespread.

The IPM study concluded that 'most of the changes in working patterns that have so far taken place have not, and probably will not, create new employment.'[21]

Further reductions in the hours of full-time workers may not, therefore, affect registered unemployment levels significantly. During the 1980s, registered unemployment in Britain became increasingly concentrated in particular areas and amongst particular groups. In most parts of the south-east, it fell rapidly, with some local labour market areas registering full employment. High levels of unfilled vacancies – for instance, in the City of London and in the commercial centre of Bristol – existed alongside high unemployment – for instance, amongst the Bengali community in Tower Hamlets and the Black communities of Brixton in south London and St Paul's in Bristol. Creating new vacancies through working time reductions will not deal with the mismatch between existing vacancies and the skills of the unemployed, nor with the problem of employers' prejudices.

In the regions and localities where high unemployment persists – usually areas which have experienced widespread redundancies and closures in manufacturing industry – there seems to be little prospect of creating a substantial number of new jobs through working time reductions in manufacturing itself. Substantially improved training and retraining programmes, investment in regional economies and the relocation of public and private sector employers all appear to be more important than cuts in working hours if regional and local unemployment is to be cut.

In Germany, reductions in the hours of full-time employees have played a far larger role in creating new jobs than extensions in part-time work. In Britain, the reverse has been the case, with the majority of new jobs filled in the last decade being part-time. Most of these part-time jobs have, of course, been filled by married women with children, most of whom were not counted as officially unemployed before taking up paid work. Indeed, a registered unemployed person who is only willing to take part-time work may disqualify himself from benefit as a result (see p.130).

Part-time jobs do not meet the income needs or aspirations of many people on the unemployment register. Nonetheless, the Labour Force Survey 1987 found over half a million unemployed people wanted part-time work.[22] In the next chapter, I look at how we could reform the social security system in order to enable people to combine part-time earnings with part-time unemployment benefit.

Controlling your own working hours

I suggested earlier that one of the objectives of working time reform – a particularly important one for individuals and their unions – is to increase people's control over their own working hours, to improve 'working time autonomy'. This may involve greater control over daily and weekly working hours, more choice about how long and when to work, greater freedom to make trade-offs between time and money, or simply the increase in leisure that comes with shorter hours at work.

Flexitime provides employees with significant working time autonomy, without requiring any change to overall working hours and without imposing costs on the organisation. Term-time working and voluntary part-time working (with *pro rata* terms and conditions) also give individual employees more choice about how long and when they work, although such arrangements may also require adjustments on the part of full-time colleagues and management.

A cut in working hours may, paradoxically, combine an increase in one kind of autonomy – more leisure – with a decrease in autonomy at the workplace. If the cut in hours is compensated for by the removal or reduction of breaks in the working day, then shorter working hours may mean greater work intensity. In many of the industrial agreements described in chapter 2, the employee gains a sharp drop in the average working week at the expense of an inflexible rostering pattern which, for instance, allocates each worker's holidays for up to a year ahead.

In some companies, unions have refused to accept work intensification in return for shorter working hours. But a high proportion of industrial workers are clearly willing to make a trade-off, particularly since shift systems have never offered a high degree of autonomy to employees, other than the ability to swap shifts with colleagues. Higher wages and shorter hours, often with longer blocks of time off, usually more than compensate for long shifts, some intensification of work practices and rostering of overtime and holidays.

In other cases, however, working time autonomy may conflict sharply with other, equally important goals. British Rail technicians have had complete freedom to trade time for money, a freedom which some used to double their income by continuous seven-day working: the cost can be a fatal accident. The requirements of health and safety must impose limits on individuals' working time freedom.

'Anti-Social' hours

The sharpest conflicts between employees and employers on working time questions usually involve evening, night and weekend work – anti-social hours. But the needs and interests of different groups of employees will not always coincide either. One person's anti-social hours may be another's conveniently flexible working time, particularly if it involves higher wages. And the consumer who wants to shop at a DIY or garden centre on a Sunday is probably also the worker who does not want to work at weekends.

The question of Sunday working and Sunday trading is reviewed later (see p.121 below). But there is a general question to be discussed here: How far is it desirable to depart from the collective, social rhythms which depend on the existence of a normal working day and a normal working week? In some towns, these community rhythms have traditionally extended to holidays, with a general shutdown during one summer week or fortnight. As one German trade union researcher points out:

> All leisure activities based on communal experience and organisation have the indispensable pre-requirement of regular periods of time that are communally available and can be communally organised.

He goes on:

> In contrast to private and domestic contacts, some areas of social life are linked to fixed times of the day. Entertainment and sporting occasions, as well as club, political or union activities usually take place at pre-arranged times which are part of a recurring, established pattern. The individual can have almost no influence on the timing of organised social activities, which have developed a pattern of their own orientated towards the 'normal working-day' . . . To the extent that working hours depart from the 'normal working week' and encroach upon the spare time belonging to the complementary area of social activities, spare time loses its useful-ness and is forced into the more stagnant areas of social life.[23]

Obviously, people working at weekends are unable to join in weekend sports and other social events.

At one extreme, if employers were permitted to impose whatever working time regimes they chose – if 'flexibility' were entirely employer led – then the pattern of social and community life could indeed be destroyed and individuals could find themselves required to work hours which were increasingly incompatible with family life and other activities.

Communication within the workplace itself becomes a problem if there is less and less time in which all employees are present. Indeed, within retailing, where individual working time contracts are becoming more common, there may well be *no* time which all employees have in common. This poses particular problems for trades unions (see chapter 8).

At the other extreme, if all or most of the workforce were working hours of their choice, including long days in return for longer weekends, or long weeks in return for longer holidays, it could become increasingly difficult to organise social and community activity – sport, the arts, meetings of local groups and so on. But individuals' preferences and decisions about the hours they work also reflect the value they themselves place on leisure, family and other activities. Since people's preferences vary, it makes more sense to give individuals a wide degree of choice about working time than to impose 'normal' working hours by regulation.

That does not mean, however, that all hours of the day and all days of the week should be treated the same by law, by management or by collective agreements. The need for breaks from work, the importance of being able to share time off with other family members and to participate in social activities, and the health and safety implications of long hours, shift work and night work all suggest that a new framework for working time should retain the concept of 'anti-social hours'.

Changing the relationship between work and family

Full-time, week-long, year-round employment is incompatible with the care of children and other dependants. The availability of men for full-time employment is not some 'natural', independent condition: it depends upon the availability of enough women to be mothers and housekeepers for nearly half of their adult working lifetime. But the availability of women for domestic work is not a 'natural', inevitable state of affairs either: it too depends upon the availability (in theory, if not always in practice) of a 'family wage' earned by men in full-time work.

But this division of paid and unpaid work, of paid and unpaid time, has changed and will go on changing as more women remain in employment after the birth of their first child or return to employment shortly afterwards and the time spent in full-time care of children is reduced. The effect of changes amongst older women are less predictable. The need to care for a growing number of very elderly people may constrain the growth in full-time employment rates amongst older women. On the other hand, a generation who have combined motherhood with part-time or full-time employment may not be willing to accept full-time domesticity. At the moment, there is strong support amongst both older and younger women for more flexible retirement.

Old policies conflict with new realities. At home, domestic responsibilities remain primarily the woman's, although, as we have seen, men are beginning to do more. At work, promotion possibilities still depend upon working full-time and more. The present situation – shorter hours of paid work and longer hours of unpaid work for women, the reverse for men – seems to be an uneasy compromise between an old pattern and a new.

But it is less clear what the new pattern will or should be. Implicit in much, although not all, of the debate about equal opportunities and about childcare seems to be the assumption that mothers should not only be enabled to stay in employment, but that they should stay in *full-time* employment. It is that view which is increasingly being challenged within the work/family debate.

A new model?

As the earlier analysis of public attitudes suggested, most women do *not* in fact want to work full-time, week in, week out, while their children are young. In the USA, despite the absence of child care, full-time employment is very high amongst women with young children. The resulting strain on both children and parents is well-documented, producing a growing interest in maternity and paternity leave, job sharing, flexitime and shorter hours working.[24]

Furthermore, it appears that a growing proportion of men would like to spend more time with their children – an aspect that was stressed in the engineering workers' campaign for a shorter working week. As we saw earlier, both women and men have actually increased the amount of time they spend in childcare over the last few decades.

Good quality childcare enhances a young child's social and intellectual development; but it is not a substitute for enabling parents themselves to choose to spend time caring for their children. Kamerman and Kahn's most recent survey suggests that childcare policies in many industrialised countries are now emphasising more time for parents as well as more nurseries for children.[25]

Furthermore, no amount of childcare provision will meet the need for other domestic work which now puts such a pressure on the 'time budgets' of full-time employees. Nor will it assist those older women and men whose working hours are severely constrained by the care of other dependent relatives.

Moving from the old model – full-time male breadwinner and full-time mother and housewife – to a new model of two full-time breadwinners relying on full-time substitute care for children and other dependants is not good enough. Enabling mothers to see as little of their children as fathers have traditionally done will not improve the lives of children, women or men.

The re-organisation of working time is therefore a vital element in the creation of a new balance between employment and family. But how should working time be changed to achieve this goal?

It is relatively easy to interrupt the dominant, full-time employment pattern by introducing *breaks* from paid work – for instance in the form of increased maternity leave, the introduction of paternity and parental leave, the development of 'career breaks' and special leave for people looking after elderly dependants.

It is much less easy, however, to identify the pattern of paid working time which best suits those with children or other dependants. Most employed mothers work part-time: should public policy encourage or inhibit the growth of part-time work?

The costs of working part-time

For most part-time workers, shorter working hours offer the best – and often, the only – way of combining employment with family responsibilities. For a smaller group, they are a gradual route or even an alternative to full-time retirement. As we have seen, part-time employees are more likely to be satisfied with their working hours and conditions than full-timers. Nonetheless the costs to these employees are very high indeed.

The recent EOC survey confirmed that part-time employment is concentrated in the service sector, particularly public services, and is more common among manual than non-manual employees. In non-manual occupations, part-time work tends to involve the less well-paid and lower status clerical and secretarial jobs. In manual occupations, part-time employees form a majority of cleaners, counter-hands, shelf assistants and other routine jobs. Nonetheless, the survey found women working part-time in almost every kind of job, including the highest grade professional and managerial jobs.[26]

It is, therefore, not surprising that a move into part-time work usually involves a drop in occupational status. The 1980 Women and Employment Survey found that one-fifth of women returning to full-time work after having their first child – and nearly half of those moving to a part-time job – had moved *down* in occupational status from their previous work.[27]

The downward mobility suffered by many women with children, particularly those working part-time, together with the lower wage rates paid to part-timers, accounts for the fact that, over their lifetime, mothers earn about 30% less than childless women. Heather Joshi has estimated that the average mother of two loses about £122,000 from her lifetime earnings – almost half her possible earnings after the age of fifteen.[28] The financial disadvantage lasts right through retirement, with those women who have previously worked part-time receiving lower occupational and state pensions or none at all.

On other terms and conditions, part-timers are also disadvantaged. The 1980 Survey found that one in five part-timers (but only one in twenty full-timers) had no paid holidays and that part-time employees were much less likely than full-timers to enjoy more than three working weeks' paid holiday. One-third had no sick pay and a further 14% did not know whether they would receive sick pay.

Just over half of full-timers, but only one in ten part-timers, belonged to an occupational pension scheme. Two-thirds of the part-timers working for an employer with a pension scheme were excluded simply because they worked part-time.

Part-time employees were also much less likely to receive training from their employers: just under half of part-timers had received some (formal or informal) training, compared with two-thirds of full-timers. Less than one in five part-timers had any opportunity for promotion in their current job; full-timers were twice as likely to have promotion opportunities.[29]

Part-time employees are also disadvantaged by the state social security system. The 1980 survey found that 40% of women part-timers paid no national insurance contributions. More recently, however, Catherine Hakim estimated that the proportion of part-time employees whose earnings were below the threshold for contributions was between one-quarter and one-third.[30] Furthermore, the unemployment benefit regulations make it difficult for even a part-time worker who has paid national insurance contributions to receive benefit if she can only take part-time work.

Discouraging part-time work?

Looking at the costs of part-time work, one might conclude that public policy should indeed promote full-time, rather than part-time, employment. There are, however, two problems with this approach. First, part-time work is popular. Second, a policy of restraining part-time employment is unlikely to work.

As we saw earlier, part-time employment is increasing rapidly even in European Community countries where it has been severely restricted. In France, where part-time work is not well-established, there is evidence of considerable demand for part-time employment amongst women.[31] The direction within the EC is clearly towards encouraging and integrating part-time employment, rather than restricting it.

The removal of discriminatory arrangements within employment law and the social security system would remove artificial incentives to create part-time jobs. But these incentives appear to have been less important in stimulating part-time employment than competitive pressures and changing production conditions.

An extension of childcare facilities in Britain would certainly enable some part-time workers who are currently working shorter hours than they would like to move back into full-time employment. But the clear preference of most part-time employees is for part-time work: and childcare provision should reflect that preference by offering far more part-time places, rather than assuming that all parents want full-time care for their children.

It is unlikely, therefore, that the extent of part-time employment will be significantly reduced by either an expansion of childcare or a change in the law. Part-time working is popular not only amongst women with children, but also amongst older workers who would like greater freedom to reduce their hours. For British employers, part-time work and other forms of non-standard working arrangements are crucial to maintaining or improving competitiveness. On both the supply and demand side, part-time working is here to stay.

Leaving policy unchanged, however, will not do either. The present discrimination against part-time employees, by government and by employers, imposes unacceptable costs and, in many cases, amounts to unlawful sex discrimination within existing British and/or European law. The House of Commons Select Committee on Employment has concluded that the distinction between part-time and full-time work is no longer useful.[32] We should aim to move beyond the part-time/full-time divide, and ensure instead that as many jobs as possible offer a range of possible working hours. The next three chapters contain detailed proposals for how government, management and unions can achieve this objective.

The six-hour day?

Would a standard, six-hour working day provide a better fit between employment and family or other activities? In Sweden, for instance, the long-term goal of the trade unions is to reduce statutory working time to six hours a day, with a thirty-hour week.[33] In Germany, the socialist party, the SPD, has adopted the target of a six-hour working day within a thirty-hour week.[34]

In both these countries, however, there is a strong tradition of regulating and standardising working hours through the law and collective bargaining, which provide vehicles for the achievement of a six-hour day. Britain has never legislated for a standard working day and the influence of collective bargaining, although still important (as the engineering workers' success demonstrates), is much weaker than it used to be. In Sweden and Germany, as well as Britain, non-standard working time arrangements are becoming far more common.

In Britain, furthermore, the six-hour day is one of the less popular options for working time change, even amongst parents. Not only do men tend to prefer a three-day weekend or extra weeks off to a shorter working day, but our research found that mothers often preferred full-time (or near full-time) working during term-times in return for school holidays off. For those with a long journey to work (men's on average being longer than women's), a six-hour/five-day week is much less efficient than an eight-hour/four-day week.

Even in Sweden and Germany, where working hours are already shorter, a six-hour day is seen as a long-term goal. In Britain, full-time working hours, particularly for men, are so long that such a target would require quite extraordinary productivity gains in order to finance it.

Where there are two employed parents in the household, the picture is complicated by the need to co-ordinate both paid work and family responsibilities. Growing working time flexibility could also make it more, rather than less difficult for parents to organise time with each other and with children.

If 'flexibility' means unpredictability – for instance, with one or both partners not knowing week by week whether or when they will be working – then childcare becomes almost impossible to organise. But 'flexibility' can also involve increasing the range of working-time choices, so that employed parents can reach more satisfactory trade-offs between time and money than they can today. As Sara Horrell points out: 'a range of different types of working regimes should be allowed to exist side by side, wherever that is technically possible, to provide opportunities for individuals to choose worktime regimes to suit their own preferences and household circumstances.'[35]

Part-time work and family income

If part-time work is to be encouraged, however, how are people to earn a decent living? After all, part-time jobs rarely offer a salary that will support one person, let alone a family. But the picture is more complicated. Certainly a lone parent would need to supplement part-time earnings with maintenance and/or benefits in order to support herself and her family (see p.128 below for the necessary reform to the social security system). But a single person without dependent children, who has perhaps already paid off a mortgage, may also be able to live on part-time earnings.

For people with children, the impact of part-time earnings depends crucially on the income available to the whole household. A family where both or all the adults are low-paid or unemployed will be forced to supplement their income from benefits, increased hours and/or informal earnings. But a low-paid, part-time worker is not necessarily part of a low-paid family. The woman's part-time earnings are often the key factor in lifting the family out of poverty. Furthermore, if the family includes at least one well-paid, full-time worker, and if those earnings are shared within the whole family – something which is not always the case[36] – then one individual's low earnings will not mean a low personal standard of living. But where the better-off partner – usually the man – fails to share his income, then part-time earnings together with child benefit become vital to the woman.

There are, as we know, financial costs for the woman who works part-time, as well as problems of economic dependency on her partner. But the rapid growth in dual-income families does not necessarily require two *full-time* workers. In 1989, the average income of a family where both partners worked was just under one-and-a-half times that of a family where only one worked. (For couples with children and one earner, the average earnings were £320; for couples with two earners, average earnings were £460.)[37] Instead of one-and-a-half workers (a man working full-time and a woman working part-time) earning one-and-a-half incomes, the same total income could in theory be produced by two three-quarters workers – a man and a woman both working shorter than full-time hours.

In practice, of course, persistent barriers to equal pay mean that most couples would be somewhat worse off, since reducing the man's employment time would cost more than reducing the woman's. But as more women gain access to training, qualifications and higher-paid jobs, the possibility of such trade-offs within families becomes more realistic.

Strong family structures, in which incomes are fully shared and time-money trade-offs negotiated between family members at different stages of the family life-cycle, may be best placed to take advantage of the flexible working patterns which are developing in post-industrial societies. Where the largest income is not shared, or where both partners are trapped in insecure and low-paid employment, part-time employment needs to be supplemented by the benefit system – and by labour market policies – if it is to contribute to an adequate standard of living.

Men can benefit too

Working time changes have already begun to contribute to a new balance between work and family. But these changes have been almost entirely confined to women.

The present direction of policy assumes that family responsibilities should continue to fall on women; that employers should be encouraged to develop special measures, including flexible hours, which will enable women to combine employment and family a little more easily; and that this in turn will increase women's employment levels and help to 'defuse the demographic time bomb'. It is rare indeed to hear politicians, employers or trades unionists suggest that if women are to do more in the workplace, then men must do more in the home.

It is not only or mainly *women's* employment which affects families. Long working hours for men reflect and reinforce social assumptions about a father's unimportance – except as the breadwinner. But children need emotional as well as financial support from their fathers. If men are denied the time to develop close bonds with their children while they are still young, it is scarcely surprising that so many lose contact with their children after separation or divorce. Whatever the family structure, children benefit emotionally and intellectually from close relationships with both their parents: and most men welcome the challenge and joy which fatherhood offers.[38]

Men who enjoy close relationships with their family and the time for active leisure are also more likely to thrive in retirement than workaholics. As we saw from our discussion groups, older men who were sceptical about many working time innovations nonetheless became enthusiastic about the idea of changing their own hours in their 50s and early 60s, perhaps working a three- or four-day week which would give them more time for DIY and other hobbies.

Thus, a policy for work and family should not only enable women to be good earners as well as good mothers: it must also enable men to be good fathers as well as good workers.

Equal opportunities at work

New working time arrangements confined to women are only a partial solution in the home. They are also a cause of problems in employment.

Equal opportunities in employment – enabling women as well as men to make the best use of their abilities – will not be achieved by creating a 'mummy track' of special working conditions for women with children.[39] Women should not have to move down the occupational ladder, losing seniority and promotion prospects, in order to obtain the working hours which they want, and which their children as well as their partners need them to have. Even if part-time work is occasionally offered to highly-qualified women in senior positions, one or two part-timers in a department run on traditional full-time lines are usually sidelined.

The issue can be stated more strongly: equal opportunities in employment is inconsistent with the male organisation of working time. As Peter Moss of the Thomas Coram Institute puts it: 'At present, the great majority of men take a minor share of childcare and other family responsibilities. The reverse side of this is their pattern of work – long hours, with much overtime; unbroken employment throughout adult life, with just a week or two off work when a child is born; and a readiness to work irregular or unpredictable hours which ignore the routines required by children and other dependents. This pattern of work sets expectations and standards which make it hard for women to compete on equal terms. Women are faced by two options – compete on men's terms, despite carrying a greater load of family responsibilities; or seek employment that is less demanding but offers fewer opportunities for development and advancement.'[40]

If the costs of *un*equal opportunities were only borne by women, we might expect them to be ignored with equanimity by many employers and even by political parties – although the need to win women's votes should persuade them otherwise. But the costs of inequality fall on everyone. Women lose out when family responsibilities prevent them from using their abilities to the full, or when combining family and highly responsible employment imposes severe personal and family stress. Children lose out when their mother becomes stressed or depressed. Employers lose out when they are unable to retain skilled or qualified women employees. And the economy as a whole loses from the under-utilisation of women's abilities.

Getting strategies for equal opportunities right is, therefore, a matter of economic as well as social necessity. And equal opportunities policies will not work without a new approach to men's as well as women's working time.

A radical vision of working time reform will not try to impose a single pattern on all employees regardless of their personal or family circumstances. Instead, we should recognise that most people want to work different hours at different stages of their lives. Our aim should be to increase the opportunities available to do so, with as many jobs as possible offering a variety of working hours and working time arrangements. People who want to change their working time should no longer have to change their jobs as well.

6 FAIR FLEXIBILITY: CHANGING THE LAW

As I argued in the last chapter, we now have an opportunity to transform working time in order to meet four goals: protecting health and safety; increasing economic efficiency; giving people more control over their own time; and reducing the conflict between work and family. In this chapter, I look at how the law needs to be changed to help achieve these goals and reconcile the conflicts between them. What does the European Community's new directive on working time mean for Britain? Do we need our own Working Time Act? What changes are needed to employment law? Should we reform the Sunday trading laws and, if so, how? Can the social security system be transformed to help part-time as well as full-time workers?

Some people argue that the government should not even try to reform working time: 'the market' will deliver whatever changes employers and employees want. There are two main reasons why this argument is wrong.

First, government will inevitably make assumptions and stipulations about working time – for instance, in the social security system and employment law. If you claim unemployment benefit, for instance, you must be available for full-time work. If you work below fifteen hours a week, you receive less legal protection than if you work twenty hours a week. And so on. Social security and employment law in Britain penalise some working time arrangements and protect others.

In other words, public policy itself creates and shapes the market in working time: and if it has created one kind of working time market today, it can create a different one tomorrow.

In any case, we are being forced by developments in the European Community to introduce new regulations about working time in Britain. The Europeanisation of the labour market through the Single Market programme has given a new impetus to attempts by the European Community to create a level playing field on working time issues as well as a range of other employment matters. Britain, with little tradition of statutory regulation of working time, will now be required by European developments to change its law.

Table 6.1 Working time regulation in Europe

		Legislation	
		Regulated	Unregulated
Collective Bargaining	Strong	Germany France Netherlands Belgium Ireland Italy Spain	Denmark
	Weak	Portugal Greece	Britain

The second reason for intervention is, quite simply, that government has a responsibility to protect people from avoidable danger. Very long working hours may create health and safety risks: government has an interest in protecting both the individual employee and others who might be affected by agreements reached between employers and employees. (To use the language of the market again, working time agreements may create externalities which can only be corrected by state action.) The public interest in the welfare of children also justifies intervention in working hours, for instance on maternity leave and time off for ante-natal care.

By definition, flexibility cannot be imposed by law. But legal changes can remove disincentives to flexibility, protect individuals against excesses of flexibility and encourage flexibility where it is most urgently needed – for employees with family responsibilities. The proposals made here are designed to give Britain a legal framework for 'fair flexibility' which will be good for employees, efficient for business and compatible with our European obligations.

Bringing Britain up to European standards

Laws and collective agreements on working hours vary considerably within the countries of the European Community. But Britain is unique in having neither general legal limits nor strong and widespread collective agreements. The position is summarised in Table 6.1.[1]

In every EC country except Denmark and Britain, working hours are closely regulated by law. By contrast, Denmark and Britain have traditionally regarded working time as a matter for collective bargaining, supplemented in Britain by protective legislation covering women and children, as well as specific industries such as mining. But the Conservative government has repealed virtually all this protective legislation, often denouncing ILO Conventions in order to do so, and removed the power of the remaining Wages Councils to regulate hours and holidays.[2]

In Denmark, most employees are covered by legally enforceable agreements reached between national employers' associations and national trades unions, supplemented in some cases by regional or local agreements. But in Britain, changes in the composition of the workforce and the shift from manufacturing to service employment have combined with new trade union legislation to weaken the impact of collective bargaining. Thus, despite the success of the engineering unions, the working hours of several million British employees are regulated neither by law nor by collective agreement.

The new European directives

Britain, however, will no longer be able to remain outside the European tradition of working time regulation. In June 1992, after two years of argument, EC Ministers agreed a compromise proposal for a new European directive on working time. Disputes between Germany and France about technical details mean that legislation will not be finalised for several months. Nonetheless, despite the British Government's longstanding opposition to the proposals – which it denounced as 'arbitrary and misguided' – and threats to challenge the legal basis of the directive, the Major Government is now committed to a directive which requires it to legislate on working hours.

This is an astonishing outcome for a government which has preached social deregulation in Europe and practised it at home. At the European Summit in Maastricht in December 1991, the British Government insisted on opting out of the social chapter, leaving the other eleven Community members free to determine legislation on social questions which would not affect the United Kingdom. The working time directive, however, is based on Article 118A of the Treaty of Rome, endorsed by Britain in the Single European Act of 1985, which permits qualified majority voting on health and safety issues. Despite the opt-out from the social chapter, therefore, Britain faced the possibility that new conditions on working hours would be imposed by a majority vote under longstanding European Treaty provisions.

The working time directive specifies:

- a 48-hour working week, including overtime;
- a minimum rest period of 11 consecutive hours in each day;
- at least 35 consecutive hours off each week;
- 4 weeks' paid holiday a year;
- no more than 8 hours' night work in a shift (averaged over 14 days);
- a ban on overtime by night workers doing hazardous or strenuous jobs.

The 48-hour week provoked the greatest fury from the British Government, which argued that it would affect about 2.5 million employees and cost firms about £5 billion in lost output or additional employment. These estimates apparently ignored the extensive provisions in the earlier drafts of the directive to exempt certain industries and to permit collective agreements with trade unions to override the limits, provided that proper protection was given to workers' health and safety.

In addition to these exemptions, however, the new Employment Secretary, Gillian Shepherd, also secured a partial opt-out from the 48-hour week. For a transitional period of ten years – which could be extended even further – British employees will be able to volunteer to work for more than 48 hours a week. Their names would have to be registered by employers and made available to the health and saftety inspectorate who could intervene if overwork was apparently causing ill-health. Following these negotiations, Mrs Shepherd proclaimed: 'We've won.'[3]

But the victory is a victory for regulation, not for deregulation. Once agreement has been reached on the number of months over which the 48-hour week should be averaged, the directive will require *all* member states, including Britain, to legislate by 1995. For the first time, all British employees will become entitled to minimum daily and weekly rest periods. Furthermore, people who do not wish to work more than 48 hours a week will have to be given legal protection against employers who try to impose longer hours. From 1999, all employees will be entitled to at least four weeks' paid annual holidays.

A new Working Time Act

The European directive will require Britain to guarantee certain minimum standards. The legislation required by the directive provides an opportunity to create a new framework for fair flexibility in Britain. Since it is neither desirable nor possible to legislate for a huge variety of working situations, the law should provide a general framework giving all employees a basic floor of working time rights, but allowing for variations through collective agreement or with the approval of the Health and Safety Executive or the Wages Councils.

The existence of exemptions does not negate the purpose of working hours legislation. The standards which the law sets should be regarded as desirable objectives as well as individual entitlements. An employee who wants to work for longer than the law permits, and whose employer wants him or her to do so, will not invoke the provisions of the law in any case. Managers, MPs and other professionals who insist on working long hours themselves generally enjoy considerable control over their working time and may regard their work as at least as much a pleasure as the rest of their lives. New legislation cannot force them to go home earlier, although it may strengthen the position of those individuals (and their families) who do want shorter hours.

No law can ban workaholism. But it can and should protect individuals – particularly those without a trade union – against employers who want to impose long hours; to permit the authorities to intervene where health and safety is threatened; and to create new social standards towards which employers and employees can move in ways which best suit their enterprise.

Because working time legislation – particularly for men – is so unusual in Britain, it is important to specify in some detail what the practical effects of both European and national regulation would be. Proposals for a new Working Time Act have been made by Bob Hepple and I have drawn on his report for much of what follows.[4]

The thirteen-hour day

The EC's proposed requirement of an eleven-hour daily rest period – in other words, a maximum thirteen-hour working day – would affect a significant minority of employees and employers. The Equal Opportunities Commission found that one in ten men had worked at least one shift of thirteen hours or more in the survey week.[5] Many of them, however, work in oil rigs, distribution and transport, where the directive permits exemptions.

A thirteen-hour limit to the average working day is clearly justified in the interests of health and safety, family life and individual autonomy and should be included in a new Working Time Act. Such a limit would still permit the innovative shift arrangements and compressed working

109

weeks described in chapter 2. The new Act should therefore allow collective agreements to lengthen the working day, but only on the basis of comprehensive health and safety provisions which meet the needs of the particular enterprise. Junior doctors and other health workers who regularly work more than thirteen hours a day (see above, p.86) would need to be covered by such an agreement.

A day-and-a-half off

Earlier drafts of the directive did not specify that the weekly rest period of 35 hours should be taken at weekends. The German Government, however, reflecting that country's tradition of strict working hours regulation, urged that Sunday should be the normal day of rest throughout the Community. That proposal, which would have affected a large and growing number of British employees, has been replaced by an agreement that each country can decide whether or not Sunday should be included in the normal weekly rest period.

Despite the absence of working hours legislation in Britain, some protection is available under employment law against coercive Sunday working. In October 1991, a seed-packer who was dismissed after refusing to work twelve hours a day, seven days a week during the harvest period won his action for unfair dismissal. His request to have Sunday off to spend time with his daughters and to go to church had been consistently rejected by his employers, a subsidiary of Unilever. The industrial tribunal decided that it was unreasonable for an employee to be given orders to damage his health and safety, which included the destruction of family life.[6]

As I argue below (see p.121), Sunday trading law should be reformed to permit more shops to open, while still protecting employees against being forced to work at weekends. Subject to that change and the usual exemptions, the new Working Time Act should give all employees the right to include Sunday in their consecutive weekly 35-hour break. Those employees exempted from the Sunday provision would, of course, still be entitled to their break at some other point in the week.

An average working week of 5½ days, as provided for in the directive, can hardly be regarded as onerous in a country where nearly 8 out of 10 people work a 5-day week or less.[7] There may even be a danger that a longer working week could be presented as the new European norm. Instead, both in Britain and within the European Community, every effort should be made to move towards the provision of an average weekly break of two days – even if the 'week end' does not always come on Saturday and Sunday.

The forty-eight-hour week

The 35-hour break, coupled with the 13-hour limit on the average working day, could still permit a 78-hour working week (six 13-hour days). But European legislation will also specify a maximum 48-hour working week. The draft directive proposed that the 48 hours be averaged across three months, although agreement on this point has not yet been reached between the Germans who want a six-month averaging period and the French who want no more than four.

In practice, the directive could still allow extremely long working weeks and days. A 48-hour week averaged over a fortnight could, at the extreme, allow one 78-hour week followed by one of 18 hours. The 48-hour week could, of course, be averaged over a far longer period – say, an entire year. In that case, the working year, allowing for four weeks' holiday, would be 2,304 hours. Assuming that no exemptions had been negotiated to the 35-hour and 11-hour breaks, a 2,304 working year could be compressed into about seven months of 78-hour weeks. If other exemptions permitted the entire working year to be compressed into six months of six-day weeks, it would require a working day of nearly 15 hours. These are deliberately extreme examples, which nonetheless illustrate the problems of working hours legislation.

At the European level, the period over which the 48-hour week is calculated should be as short as possible, thus providing reasonable protection for employees. Exemptions to meet the needs of different enterprises should be sought through collective bargaining, or other arrangements approved by health and safety authorities, rather than through a long averaging period.

In addition, as we have seen, British employees will be allowed to volunteer for a longer working week. Presumably, however, they will not be allowed to volunteer away their other entitlements. The 35-hour weekly break, together with the 11-hour daily rest, together permit an average working week of 78 hours.[8] This appears to represent the limit which the present government is prepared to accept on individuals' voluntary working hours. But there will be no limit on the hours worked under *collective* agreements, provided that they include adequate provisions for health and safety.

Collective agreements have the great merit that they provide a formal framework for a trade-off between the interests of employees and those of employers where these conflict. For instance, annual hours contracts can allow employers to cope with big seasonal variations by averaging long hours in one part of the year against short hours for the remainder. Such arrangements suit some people, but can be highly disruptive for others. The Confederation of Engineering and Shipbuilding Workers, for instance, has found real resistance to annualisation of this kind from members who travel to work with their partners – something which depends on different enterprises in the same area having similar shift hours. At the same time, the efficiency gains from seasonal hours working can be very considerable. Collective bargaining can allow conflicts of this kind to be resolved, particularly where different arrangements can be agreed for different workplaces and where local agreements give the greatest possible choice to individual employees.

The irony is that a government so hostile to trade unions has been forced by its own Single European Act into legislation which will, in practice, encourage employers to enter into collective agreements which can amend the basic legal standards in order to meet the circumstances of their particular enterprise. A further inducement may be provided by what appear to be rather bureaucratic arrangements for recording all individuals opting out of the 48-hour week.

The British government's proposal to allow the health and safety authorities to intervene where employees' health may be at risk is, however, welcome. It should be strengthened to allow intervention where there is a danger of risk to the *public*, as well as to the employees – as in the case of air traffic controllers, doctors or the British Rail signals engineers.

Eight-hour shifts

The directive restricts night workers to eight hours in any 24. But because the hours can be averaged over a 14 day period, the provision is not quite what it seems. Allowing for weekly rest periods, the directive would in fact allow up to eight night shifts of 12 hours, or seven shifts of 13 hours, in any one fortnight (giving a total of about 96 hours' night work) Thus, the present draft would appear to permit the innovative shift work arrangements described in chapter 2. In addition, management and unions have even greater flexibility in establishing collective agreements which produce long rest periods as well as productivity gains.

Four weeks' holidays

Alone in the Community, Britain provides no legal right to paid holidays. Although the directive's requirement for four weeks' holidays does not need to be implemented until 1999, the new legislation should include an immediate entitlement to four weeks' paid holiday within each year of service.

The costs to employers would be very small, since the vast majority of full-time employees already receive at least four weeks' paid holiday. The benefit would be felt by the minority of workers – mainly part-timers – who are currently disadvantaged. (For part-time employees, the holiday period would of course be *pro rata*.)

Some employers, long accustomed to an absence of regulation in Britain, may fear that such legislation would impose intolerable costs. The evidence of present working arrangements suggests, however, that such fears are unfounded particularly given the scope for exemptions. It must also be recognised that, especially in small and non-unionised workplaces, individual employees may choose to ignore their basic rights. Nonetheless, minimum protection should be offered to everyone and the proposals described above represent a reasonable compromise between the interests of employers and those of employees.

Full-time rights for part-time employees

The laws dealing with unfair dismissal, redundancy pay, statutory sick pay, paid maternity leave, and so on, create a jumble of qualifying conditions based on hours of work. Although some rights apply to everyone, there are basically three groups of employees: those working 16 hours or more a week who receive the greatest protection provided they have been employed for a minimum period, generally two years; those working between 8 and 15 hours a week who generally only qualify after they have been with their employer for five years; and those working less than 8 hours, who have almost no rights. Because 'continuous service' is required in most cases, new working time arrangements – such as week on/week off, term time and annual hours working and zero hours contracts – may leave the employee completely unprotected.[9]

It is popularly believed that part-time employees are generally excluded from employment law, and that this is one of their major attractions for employers. In fact, the 1980 Women and Employment Survey found that women part-time employees were nearly as likely as women full-timers to qualify for employment protection (60% of part-timers, compared with 67% of full-timers).[10] Since then, the level of protection amongst part-time employees has declined. Catherine Hakim estimated from the 1986 Labour Force Survey that one-half of women part-time employees, compared with two-thirds of women full-timers and three-quarters of male full-timers, were covered by the law. She suggested that, with the 1980s rise in part-time jobs, many new part-time workers had not yet been able to stay in their work for the necessary two or five years' continuous service to qualify for legal protection.[11] It appears, however, from the EOC survey in 1989 that the proportion of part-time employees protected by the law has continued to decline, to 40–45% of part-timers compared with about 60% of women full-timers. This change reflects the drop in the hours worked by part-timers (see p.21 above). Overall, the EOC found that just over one-half of all women employees were covered by the law, compared with over two-thirds of men.[12]

Despite these significant inequalities, part-time employment does not allow employers to escape their obligations under employment law. A second EOC survey of employers' use of flexible labour concluded that, even today, reduced employment protection is not the primary reason for a greater use of part-time employment: 'Changes in hours seemed to be more related to specific establishment requirements than to the opportunities to reduce costs offered by the current hours' limits of the employment protection laws and earning limits for national insurance contributions. When asked about the proposed changes in employment protection laws or indeed any future changes in national innsurance thresholds, only five of our interviewees said that such changes were likely to affect their use of part-time workers.'[13]

The Equal Opportunities Commission has tried, so far without success, to challenge these qualifying periods in the European Court of Justice on the grounds that they indirectly discriminate against women and are therefore contrary to the existing directive on equal treatment. In other draft directives on part-time and temporary workers, the European Commission has proposed that all employees with an average working week of eight hours or more should be covered by statutory and occupational social security schemes and by employment law.

A general eight-hours threshold has many advantages over the present patchwork. In order to embrace most of the new working time contracts, the average would need to be calculated over a lengthy period. It would, however, continue to exclude almost half a million British employees from legal protection. And unless the system of national insurance contributions were reformed, many low-paid workers who would be brought within the protection of the system could also find themselves having to pay contributions (see below, p. 128, for a further discussion of national insurance and social security).

In 1989, the Labour Party proposed extending employment protection rights to all employees regardless of their hours of work or how long they have been employed.[14] This approach has the great merit of simplicity and consistency. It could, however, give rise to practical problems of enforcement; the original justification for a qualifying period was to ensure that industrial tribunals were not overwhelmed by small claims. It would also be unpopular with employers.

The European Commission justifies its own proposed threshold on the grounds of avoiding 'disproportionate administrative costs'. As a first step, Britain should adopt the EC proposal for employment protection law, but ensure that the eight hours can be averaged over several months and applies to hours actually worked rather than to those nominally contracted.

Since the majority of British employees are already covered by employment laws, lowering the hours threshold in this way will not impose excessive additional costs on employers. And the evidence from employers themselves, as well as from the present impact of employment law, is that there is no foundation for Conservative Ministers' fears that part-time employees would lose their jobs if employers were required to treat them fairly.

The equal treatment principle

As we have seen, employment law creates one set of dividing lines between different groups of part-time and full-time employees. Employers' own policies create another. Membership of occupational pension and sick pay schemes, access to training and promotion opportunities and so on vary substantially between enterprises. But as I explained in chapter 5, part-time employees consistently do less well.

Employers usually justify discrimination against part-timers on the grounds that they are less committed employees. The Institute of Personnel Management points out, however, that 'the overall level of absenteeism and turnover of part-time staff is often not markedly lower than that of their full-time counterparts, and there is certainly a strong logic to the argument that if pension schemes were extended to part-time workers, it would considerably increase the job security of the positions involved, and therefore encourage a greater degree of commitment.'[15]

Since this IPM guide was published seven years ago, a growing number of employers have extended full-time conditions, *pro rata*, to their permanent part-time staff. And a new study by the Institute of Manpower Studies, commissioned by IBM, Shell, the Post Office and other large employers, found that staff working part-time, flexible hours or job-sharing were considered by their employers to be 'more efficient, enthusiastic and committed' than their full-time equivalents.[16]

Discrimination against part-time employees in their terms and conditions of employment has been challenged under British sex discrimination and equal pay laws and, in the European Court, under the Treaty of Rome and the EC's Equal Treatment Directive. As Professor Hepple stresses, however, the law does not help those part-timers who are in female ghettoes of unskilled and semi-skilled jobs, because there is no male employee with whom they can compare themselves, and recent rulings still leave employers considerable scope for justifying discrimination.[17]

The principle of equal treatment of part-time and full-time employees was set out in the European Commission's draft directive in 1983 and is included in the 1990 draft on part-time and temporary employment. Unlike the 1983 draft, however, the 1990 draft does not cover wages and other employment matters such as access to promotion or job content; it is restricted to national and occupational social security schemes, holidays, dismissal and seniority allowances.

The basis for this change is that, in the Commission's view, differences in wages do not restrict competition within the Community since they are usually compensated for by productivity. By contrast, 'indirect wage costs', including social security contributions set by government, restrict competition and therefore undermine the Single Market programme. Thus, the Commission is seeking to correct the situation where, for instance, a company employing someone for below fifteen hours a week in the Netherlands must also pay social security contributions, but would pay no contributions for an employee working the same hours on the same wage in Germany.[18] According to the principle of subsidiarity, wage matters should be left to collective bargaining, but discrimination in indirect wage costs should be regulated on a Community basis.

The Commission may come under pressure to strengthen its draft directives on the treatment of part-time workers. If, however, the directive is implemented in its present form, British part-time employees will be left in a thoroughly unsatisfactory position, with their terms and conditions decided by a patchwork of employers' discretion; collective bargaining or Wages Councils orders; and the operation of the Sex Discrimination and the Equal Pay Acts, as modified by the requirements of European Community law. Since part-time employees are much less likely to be union members or covered by a collective agreement than full-timers, they will continue to be disadvantaged.

I have argued earlier that for both economic and social reasons, part-time working should be fully integrated with full-time working. In any case, it is increasingly difficult to distinguish legally or practically between part-time and full-time employment. The British Government should, therefore, accept the principle of equal treatment and give it statutory basis.

The equal treatment principle would require employers to give part-time employees the same wage rates and other terms and conditions of employment, on a *pro rata* basis, as full-timers. A comparison of part-time employees' wage rates could be made with full-time men or women employees performing the same work or work of equal value (a principle already accepted in equal pay legislation). Membership of occupational pension and sick pay schemes, and access to other benefits – including training and promotion – could no longer be denied on the grounds of part-time status.

Because the equal treatment principle is already accepted by a growing number of employers, its application is in most cases easy to describe. A problem arises, however, with overtime. Although it would be logical for a part-time employee to qualify for overtime rates once she worked more than her normal contracted hours, virtually no employer has taken this step and there does not appear to be a collective agreement of this kind – for the obvious reason that the part-time employee could then be paid a higher hourly rate for working the same hours (or indeed fewer hours) as a full-time employee doing the same work. Some employers pay overtime rates to a part-timer who works more than the normal full-time *daily* hours in any one day; but usually a part-timer only qualifies for overtime payment by working more than the normal full-time *weekly* hours. The issue may become less important as overtime working becomes absorbed in annual hours and other new working time agreements; indeed, many companies are recruiting part-timers in order to reduce or eliminate overtime working by full-timers. For the time being, equal treatment legislation should require overtime rates to be paid to part-timers at the same threshold as full-timers.

Employing a part-timer has traditionally been cheaper, on an hourly basis, than employing a full-timer. The IPM gives an example of a department store which calculated the real hourly cost as about 12% less than the equivalent full-timer, as a result of savings on the employer's occupational pension scheme and national insurance contributions, together with the savings on paid morning and afternoon tea breaks for which part-time staff were not eligible.[19] Since equal treatment legislation will mean an increase in wage costs for some firms, it may be desirable to phase in the equal treatment principle, to give companies time to adjust. For most employers, however, the increase in wage costs should be more than offset by further reductions in absenteeism and turnover, improved recruitment and other productivity gains.

Time off for parents

The European Commission has also proposed a draft directive on the protection of pregnant women, which would guarantee all employed mothers fourteen weeks' leave on full pay with two weeks' paid leave before confinement, regardless of how long they had worked for their employer. The draft has, however, run into disagreements between national governments and the European Parliament, backed by the European Commission, over the level of payment.

A suggested compromise, providing maternity pay at the same level as national sick pay schemes, would still leave British women well behind the standards which apply in most other EC countries. Instead, all pregnant employees should be given the right to take maternity leave for up to 40 weeks, with the right to return to employment – wherever possible, in their previous job. Six weeks' leave should be on full pay, with a further twelve weeks on maternity benefit. This provision would build on the present entitlement of up to eleven weeks' leave before the birth and up to 29 weeks afterwards. Employers' costs should continue to be reimbursed by government, so that there is no disincentive to an individual employer to take on a woman who is pregnant or might wish to become so.

The second priority is to introduce paternity leave. Most fathers take part of their holidays at the time of the child's birth. We now need to give official recognition to the importance of the father, as well as the mother, having time to form close emotional links with the new baby.[20] There is justified public concern about the effects on children of rising divorce rates and the loss of contact with one parent (usually the father) which divorce often involves. Public policy has generally emphasised the father's *financial* responsibility towards his children: now it needs to emphasise his *emotional* responsibilities as well. A statutory right to paid paternity leave – which could be set initially at a modest five working days – would mark this change.

Within the separate context of divorce and maintenance law, we should consider another step to mark the importance attached to the time parents have available with children. An absent parent can already be required to pay maintenance. As Sylvia Hewlett has suggested, absent parents (unless disqualified by violence or other abuse) should be required to spend time, as well as money, on their children.[21]

Maternity leave when the child is born should then be followed by a period of parental leave of at least three months, available to either father or mother. This leave would be unpaid, unless of course the employer or a collective agreement provided otherwise. Given the additional employment costs involved in working time legislation, an extension of maternity leave and the introduction of paternity leave, it would be reasonable to expect the new right to parental leave to be introduced within five years or so rather than at the same time as the other changes.

Part-time work for parents

As we have seen, Sweden, Finland and France all offer parents a right to reduce their working hours while children are young. Although women frequently move from full-time to part-time work after having a child, there is little experience in Britain of women who have taken maternity leave returning to the *same* job or employer on a part-time basis.

Hepple reviews the attempts which have been made to challenge the requirement to return to work full-time after maternity leave as 'indirectly discriminatory' under the Sex Discrimination Act. Although one executive officer in the Home Office succeeded in establishing her right to return part-time, the Employment Appeal Tribunal stressed that the decision rested on the particular facts of the case (the job could be done unsupervised in part-time hours) and did not set a general precedent. In a later case, an industrial tribunal ruled that a health visitor's job required a five-day week. In another case involving job-sharing by a husband and wife, the EAT held that 'in many working structures, there will be a grade or position which by its very nature requires full-time attendance' and that 'it is for the employer, acting reasonably, to decide what is required for the purposes of running his business or establishment.' Hepple concludes that there is little hope of using the present anti-discrimination law as a path to flexible working hours.[22]

The practical problems of creating a right for parents to return to work part-time are twofold. First, there is the general issue of whether any job above a certain level of seniority or responsibility can be done part-time. Although some positions will not be suitable for part-time work, even on a job-sharing basis, it is clear from the evidence in the first half of this book that far more jobs could be done in a variety of part-time ways than are available at present.

The second question is whether it is reasonable to expect employers and colleagues to accommodate two consecutive periods of maternity (or parental) leave – the first full-time, the second part-time. Most employers are now accustomed to the need to employ a temporary replacement for an employee on maternity leave who has indicated that she plans to return to work, or to re-allocate her work in some other way. Depending on the size of the enterprise and the nature of the work involved, the disruption could be much greater if, for instance, a full-time replacement had to be employed for 40 weeks and a second, part-time replacement (effectively, a job-sharer) had to be employed for a further period while the original employee worked part-time.

Employers in Sweden, who also face these problems, seem far more willing to cope with the period of full-time maternity or parental leave than with the reduced working day. Furthermore, a cut in hours may reduce the employee's occupational pension rights as well as promotion and training prospects. The private sector in Britain starts from an even lower level of acceptance of the need for a better fit between work and family, although some British public utilities and banks have found that working shorter hours is more popular with employees, and can enable them to keep up with developments at the workplace more easily, than an extended career break.[23] Extending paid leave to all pregnant women, introducing paternity and, later, parental leave will all add to the demands on management. It may be unrealistic to expect them to accept at the same time the added complications of an unqualified right to return part-time.

It may, however, be possible to introduce some limited statutory provision for part-time work after maternity/parental leave. After all, a substantial proportion of employers in this country have introduced or expanded part-time employment because it is good for business. A smaller number have demonstrated that highly flexible working arrangements, including a return to part-time working after full-time maternity leave, are not only manageable, but profitable. The PSI survey found that nearly eight out of ten employers reported offering part-time working opportunities to help mothers of young children: some, if not all, presumably included the opportunity to return to the same job, or the same level of seniority, on a part-time basis.[24]

Following the French example, therefore, Britain should introduce a new statutory right for women returning from maternity leave to return to their previous or an equivalent job part time with the employer's agreement. (A similar right would be extended to fathers at the end of parental leave.) In larger firms (the French dividing line is 100 employees), the employer could not withhold agreement; in smaller firms, agreement could be withheld if a return to part-time working would 'unreasonably' disrupt the business. Disputes could be referred to an industrial tribunal for adjudication. In order that women working in smaller firms were not unreasonably disadvantaged, a woman who was refused the right to return part-time should be entitled to an additional period (say two months) of paid full-time maternity leave.

An alternative approach would be to entitle every new parent to return to work part-time at the end of maternity/parental leave, with the proviso that she would not necessarily be entitled to return to her previous job if that would 'unreasonably' disrupt the work of the enterprise. Whatever the job to which she returns, however, she would be entitled to the same terms and conditions, on a *pro rata* basis, as she enjoyed in her previous job.

Ideally, the employee's right to return to full-time employment after a period of part-time work should be protected (as it is in the Civil Service schemes described on p.32 above). In practice, however, it may be more difficult for the employer to reorganise the work for a limited period, than on a permanent basis. Where a job-sharer is employed, to make up the hours of the new parent, it would be reasonable if the job-sharer left to give the parent the right, at that point, to return to full-time employment. Whatever approach is adopted, the parent's continuity of employment before and after the birth should be preserved.

Never on a Sunday?

Sunday working and Sunday trading raise particularly difficult questions about working time flexibility.

In Britain, with its virtual absence of working hours regulation, Sunday *working* is lawful. In theory, offices could open seven days a week with employees contractually obliged to work on a rota basis. In practice, however, Sunday working is confined to a minority, although a sub-stantial one – some 29% of employees or around 7 million people – who already work regularly or occasionally on a Sunday.[25]

In Scotland, there are no legal restrictions on Sunday trading. Sunday *trading* in England and Wales is, however, regulated by the 1950 Shops

Act which severely restricts the kind of goods which may legally be sold on a Sunday. The Act is widely breached; the willingness of local authorities to enforce its provisions varies considerably; and its validity has been challenged under European Community law.[26]

As we saw in chapter 4, most surveys of public opinion reveal wide support for liberalisation or deregulation of Sunday trading. The recommendations of the Auld Committee, which reported in 1984, for complete deregulation of Sunday trading, together with retention of Wages Councils to protect shop workers, were supported by a substantial majority in the House of Commons in 1985. The following year, the Conservative Government introduced a Bill to deregulate Sunday trading – while making clear its intention to weaken and indeed abolish the Wages Councils. Despite public and Parliamentary support for reform of the Sunday trading laws, an effective combination of shopworkers, churches, community groups and some retailers led to the Bill's defeat.

Resolution of the Sunday trading question depends upon the different interests of three groups: consumers, shop workers and the community as a whole.

For practising Christians, of course, Sunday has a special meaning. But in a society which is not only largely secular but includes a number of different religions, Christianity does not by itself provide a justification for legal restrictions on Sunday trading. There is, however, a clearly identifiable community interest in 'keeping Sunday special', in retaining one day, and indeed the weekend itself, with a different rhythm from that of the routine working week.

It is less clear, however, whether legal restrictions on trading are necessary to maintain the distinctive character of Sundays. In the 'deregulated' office sector, Sunday working is almost unknown. In Scotland (where Sunday observance laws were deemed to have fallen into disuse) and in Ireland (where Sunday trading has been lawful since 1938), the pattern is remarkably similar to that in England and Wales: a minority of stores open on Sundays throughout the year, with others joining them in the weeks before Christmas.

Public opinion surveys throughout the 1980s suggested that consumer demand for Sunday shopping remained clearly distinct from weekday demand, with the emphasis on DIY stores, garden centres, local 'convenience' stores, food supermarkets, video hire and, to a lesser extent, clothes. For most families, Sunday is no longer confined to going to church, visiting relatives and being at home (although the latter two, at least, remain popular). Shopping linked to activities at home, to family outings and to leisure are increasingly part of a normal family Sunday which remains nonetheless distinct from the rest of the week.

For those working to keep shops and other organisations open, of course, Sunday is not a leisure day, a cost which needs to be compensated for both by money and by other time off. Where Sunday shopping is highly developed as a family and leisure activity, as in many Australian cities, a new pattern is developing with the busy Saturday/Sunday weekend followed by a Monday/Tuesday or even Monday/Tuesday/Wednesday 'weekend' for traders and their employees.

For consumers, an extension of Sunday trading would offer a wider choice of shopping time. Buying goods costs time as well as money.[27] With the growing pressure on families' time budgets as both partners (or the only parent) work, the time costs of shopping increase. Those costs, and the pressure on time budgets which give rise to them, will be reduced if shopping hours are extended.

Not surprisingly, therefore, growing consumer demand for Sunday trading has paralleled the growth in married women's employment. A study commissioned by the Auld Committee from the Institute for Fiscal Studies concluded that the 'regional pattern of demand for Sunday trading follows closely the pattern of economic activity for women across Great Britain'.[28]

There would, however, be disadvantages as well as advantages for consumers in the extension of Sunday trading. The IFS study concluded that in the highly competitive retail sector, 'longer opening hours would be likely to lead to some acceleration of the trend towards the disappearance from the market place of independent traders and towards increasing concentration among multiple retailers. For consumers, greater choice of time could in some degree be offset by reduced choice of establishment'. Many people deplore these trends within the retail sector. But they have developed independently from the status of Sunday shopping: for instance, the proportion of retail workers employed in multiples rose from less than one in five in 1950 to half in 1982. It must be doubted whether a small degree of protection given to independent traders is sufficient justification for strict controls on Sunday trading – let alone for the present state of the law.

On balance, consumers' interests would be served by some liberalisation of Sunday trading, while the community's interests can be effectively protected without the present restrictions. But the interests of the third group – the shop workers themselves – are more difficult to define and protect.

Protecting shop workers

The shop workers' union, USDAW, has vigorously opposed relaxation of Sunday trading laws and pressed local authorities to enforce the 1950 Act. The union argues that, in the absence of regulation, jobs would be lost as the existing volume of trade was spread more thinly over seven days and week-day full-time employment was reduced. The quality of employment would suffer, as full-time jobs were replaced by lower-paid, part-time jobs, and low pay would increase as employers sought to compensate for the higher costs involved in longer opening hours.

The IFS study remains the most comprehensive analysis of the likely effects of shopping hours deregulation on employment. They concluded, first, that the short-term effect of removing restrictions on Sunday trading would – in the absence of any increase in the total volume of sales – be a loss of about 5,000 *full-time* jobs in retailing but an overall increase of about 5,000 employees, as a result of the substantial increase in part-time jobs. Second, they estimated an increase in total annual earnings of some £325 million, mainly as a result of double-time premia for Sunday working.

Two qualifications must be made to this statement of the IFS conclusions. First, IFS modelled the effect of moving from effective prohibition on Sunday trading to deregulation. Since the 1950 Act is only partly enforced and a significant increase in Sunday trading had already taken place, IFS stress that their conclusions overstate the actual effect of liberalising the law.

Second, the prediction of job losses depends upon the assumption that the total volume of sales would not increase as a result of Sunday trading. If in fact sales were to increase by a modest 0.5%, there would be no short-term job losses, while an increase of 1.5% would also remove the prospect of longer-term job losses.[29] The present recession has, of course, severely affected retailing employment: in more favourable economic conditions, however, it is reasonable to expect that liberalisation of Sunday trading, by reducing the 'time costs' of shopping, would help to stimulate some increase in overall sales.

The IFS study does not bear out USDAW's fears of a general increase in low pay in an already low-paid sector. It does, however, confirm the union's expectation of a shift from full-time to part-time employment. IFS's detailed modelling of the impact on earnings show an increase in annual earnings from Sunday jobs of £700 million and a further increase in earnings from weekday jobs of £125 million (to carry out clerical and other functions generated by Sunday trading), coupled with a *loss* of £500 million in earnings from weekday jobs (again, assuming no increase in sales).

The demand for additional Sunday labour generated by the growth in Sunday opening, in Scotland and elsewhere, has been met in two different ways: increased Sunday working for full-time staff; and increased employment of part-time staff, including those who work on Sunday only. Thus, the changes in earnings described by the IFS study does not simply imply a shift from full-time to part-time earners; some of the increased earnings, from Sunday as well as weekday employment, would go to full-timers. Provided Sunday working continues to be paid at premium rates, a full-time employee who substitutes Sunday work for a week day will increase her pay. But where the hours of weekday full-timers are reduced, and part-timers employed on Sunday, there will be a shift from full-time to part-time earnings.

If full-time employment is the ideal, and part-time employment an undesirable second-best, then some of the consequences of increased Sunday trading will indeed be unacceptable. But as we have seen, a significant minority of full-time employees would in fact prefer to work part-time. Some weekend work already attracts students, women with children and others for whom full-time weekday work is unattractive, impractical or both. The development of individual working hours contracts in the German retail sector (see p.46 above) suggests that if full-time employees are offered a trade-off between time and money, with a range of working hours, weekday and weekend options and appropriate premia for the less attractive hours, a match can be found between the requirements of both employees and employers.

In Scotland, too, there is no evidence that deregulation of Sunday trading has led to full-time workers being coerced into working on Sundays. There are, however, fears that removal of Wages Council protection from people under the age of 21 will encourage a growing number of firms to open on Sunday with part-time young employees who do not qualify for the Wage Council Sunday premium or indeed any minimum wage at all.[30]

Any liberalisation of Sunday trading must therefore be accompanied by a re-regulation of working conditions. Defeat of the 1986 Bill was largely prompted by the present Government's failure to accept the Auld Committee's trade-off between Sunday trading deregulation and main-tenance of the retail sector Wages Council, and their inclusion in the Bill of a provision designed to protect existing employees from compulsory Sunday working which the Auld Committee had already rejected as unworkable. One member of the Auld Committee, Frances Cairncross, has said recently that: 'No liberalisation of shopping hours is likely to succeed unless it offers shopworkers some kind of protection, even if only of a transitional sort.'[31]

Opponents of Sunday trading sometimes suggest that legal protection for shopworkers will be unenforceable. Legal protection is never perfect: many people who have succeeded in winning a case for unfair dismissal still fail to win their jobs back. Taking a case to an industrial tribunal also costs time and money. But there is no reason why laws for shopworkers should be any less satisfactory than other employment protection. Indeed, the recent industrial tribunal decision in favour of a man dismissed for refusing to work on Sundays (see p.110 above) offers some hope that tribunals will be sympathetic to claims under new legislation on Sunday trading. That legislation should be designed to ensure that Sunday working is performed by volunteers, that conscientious objectors are protected and that Sunday working continues to attract special rates.

The reasonably optimistic picture provided by the IFS analysis depends upon its assumption that Sunday work will continue to be paid at double rates. In Scotland, for instance, USDAW has negotiated a 100% premium for Sunday working with Tesco. Since many retail workers are not unionised, however, it would be unwise to assume that Sunday premia will persist in the face of growing liberalisation. Requiring employers to pay a Sunday premium would protect employees against a worsening of their working conditions and, more generally, confirm the special status of Sunday working. Statutory protection should therefore be given to retail employees, both through a strengthened retail sector Wages Council and through a statutory requirement for a Sunday premium. Shop workers would also, of course, be protected by the general provisions in a Working Time Act on maximum weekly hours and daily and weekly rest periods.

In practice, employers both in Scotland and in England and Wales have generally been able to recruit Sunday staff without compulsion, preferring for obvious reasons to use volunteers. Protecting the legal position of existing employees would not, therefore, cause employers practical difficulties and would protect individuals against an undesirable form of 'flexibility'. Legal protection would also be needed against an unscrupulous employer who sought to terminate all existing contracts in order to offer fresh contracts which required Sunday working. Thus, legislation should provide that no employee could be required to work on a Sunday except with her or his voluntary agreement; that any dismissal or victimisation for refusing to work on a Sunday would be unlawful;

and that no employee could be required to accept a change in his employment contract requiring Sunday working. Legal protection should also be extended to those who have a conscientious objection against Sunday working.

These measures would not, however, prevent the development of new full-time contracts which required employees to be available for Sunday working 'as and when required'. In practice, people seeking retail jobs would have little or no choice about accepting such conditions. Nor would they prevent the growth of part-time Sunday jobs at the expense of full-time jobs.

It would be technically possible to make it unlawful for employers to require Sunday working as a condition of offering full-time employment, thus reinforcing the principle that Sunday working by full-timers should be voluntary. Such a requirement might, however, simply speed up the growth of Sunday-only and other part-time jobs. Nor would it be possible to outlaw new contracts for part-time work which required Sunday working, since such contracts – which are usually entered into by volunteers – are necessary to meet at least some of the Sunday work involved in liberalisation. It would also create a new distinction between full-time and part-time employees, contrary to the general principle of equal treatment, and is therefore best omitted.

The Code of Practice for Sunday working in shops published in January 1991 by the Shopping Hours Reforms Council covers the three central points just referred to. It would, however, only apply to companies who chose to subscribe to it and should therefore be used as a basis for legislation, and not a substitute.

Provided employment protection is offered along these lines, there remains the question of whether Sunday trading should be completely deregulated or only partly liberalised. The Adam Smith Institute has argued for a completely free market in Sunday trading and concluded that 'any half-way solution would probably produce further anomalies'.[32] The experience of Ireland and Scotland suggest that complete deregulation would not in fact wipe out the special character of Sunday. Nonetheless, caution is justified. Not only would it be difficult to create a public and Parliamentary consensus for deregulation, but there are real difficulties – the vulnerability of shopworkers and the environmental problems caused by extended shopping hours – which need to be tackled. Any government willing to attempt reform again would be well advised to restrict the legalisation of Sunday trading to a limited category of shops and to combine that measure with strong legal protection for shopworkers linked to a new Working Time Act.

National insurance and social security

The national insurance system was designed in the 1940s to protect people who would be in full-time employment throughout their working lives – in other words, men and single women. It was not intended to accommodate women whose family responsibilities would interrupt their employment; its architect, William Beveridge, always envisaged that a married woman would only qualify for benefit through her husband's contributions. Nor was it designed to replace *part-time* earnings or to cope with increasingly varied, non-standard employment contracts. The contributory principle at the heart of national insurance was built on a 'standard' – that is, male – employment relationship.

Payment of benefit in return for contributions was supplemented by a system of means-tested benefits which, although originally intended as a safety-net for a small minority, has assumed a far greater importance in recent years. In 1985, the government initiated the 'Fowler Review' of social security, designed to create a social security system which could take Britain into the 21st century. But, as Ruth Lister has stressed, the Review signally failed to address the transformation of women's lives at home and at work over the previous forty years.[33]

Today's system of contributory and means-tested benefits is complex, internally contradictory, under-funded and unable to cope with new labour market realities. The fundamental re-appraisal which it requires is the subject of another IPPR study, by Lynda Bransbury.[34] Here I briefly consider, from the perspective of working hours, some of the problems which need to be tackled and the principles which should govern reform.

Under the national insurance system, all employees whose earnings are above the 'lower earnings limit' are required to pay national insurance contributions which, in turn, help them to qualify for unemployment and other benefits and retirement pension. Employers are also required to contribute.

National insurance contributions are effectively a form of income tax, although one that is directly related to benefit entitlement. But they currently become payable at a *lower* level of earnings than income tax. Once the lower earnings limit has been reached, contributions are paid at 2% on all earnings below the limit and 9% on earnings above. After the tax threshold is reached, the combined rate of national insurance contributions and income tax is initially 29% (reflecting the reduced rate tax band introduced in the 1992 Budget), but moves rapidly to 34%. For employers, a different set of thresholds apply, with contributions moving from an initial 5% to 10.45% for higher earnings.

The result is a substantial disincentive to *both* employees and employers to increase (declared) earnings over the limits at which national insurance contributions become payable. By keeping official earnings below the lower earnings limit, an employer avoids the bureaucracy and administrative costs involved in both national insurance and PAYE. The employee avoids paying contributions or income tax – something welcomed by many low-paid women and men who want to maximise earnings and minimise involvement with bureaucracy. But they also forego entitlement to future unemployment, sickness, invalidity and maternity benefit, and jeopardise their retirement pension. About two million people – between one-quarter and one-third of part-time workers and around one in a hundred full-time self-employed or employed workers – fall below the lower earnings limit.[35]

The European Commission's proposed hours threshold would require anyone employed for eight hours or more a week to be protected by the national insurance system. The British Government has criticised the proposal on the grounds that it would require low-paid workers to pay contributions and, by increasing employers' costs, would reduce part-time employment. An hours threshold, without any regard for earnings, would also make it possible for a highly-paid self-employed consultant, who can earn several hundreds of £s for a few hours' work, to be exempted from contributions.

It appears, however, that the draft directive is not intended to create such anomalies. Its purpose – of securing social security protection for part-time employees – could be met by exempting employees with hours above the threshold but earnings below the limit from contributions, while crediting them into the system in the same way that an unemployed claimant is currently awarded contribution credits. In order to protect people whose working weeks vary considerably, the eight hours' minimum needs to be averaged over a longer period of, say, six months or a year.

The government's fears that part-time work would dry up as a result of the directive appear equally ill-founded. Over two-thirds of part-time employees already have earnings above the national insurance threshold and over half earn above the income tax threshold.[36] The desire of employers and employees to avoid contributions and tax is far less important in explaining the rise of part-time employment than employers' need to match labour to peaks and troughs of demand and employees' needs for more convenient working hours. In so far as the national insurance and tax thresholds influence employers and employees, they create an incentive to hold down (declared) earnings and, thus, to hold down working hours without reference to the actual requirements of either business and worker.

Benefits for the unemployed

In more recent years, the qualifying conditions for national insurance benefits have been significantly tightened, with the result that even some of those who have been in full-time employment throughout their working lives can fail to qualify for benefit, for instance because their contributions record is defective as a result of irregular work, especially if they are low paid. Furthermore, entitlement to some benefits, such as unemployment benefit, is linked to behaviour in a traditional working week, Sunday to Sunday. It can, therefore, be very difficult for someone employed on an annual hours or term-time contract to prove they are 'unemployed' in any particular week.

The central issue to be considered here is the relationship between employment – whether full-time or part-time – and benefits for unemployment. Such benefits are of two kinds: unemployment benefit, based on national insurance contributions, and income support, based on a test of means. Different rules apply to each benefit. In order to focus on the issues of principle involved, I have deliberately simplified the description of the rules which follows.

Someone who loses their job – whether part-time or full-time – must show that they are 'available for work' in order to qualify for unemployment benefit. There is no specific requirement to be available for *full-time* work; there is no mention in the regulations of minimum weekly hours; and benefit is payable for each day of unemployment. Despite this apparent flexibility, however, benefit will be refused if a claimant restricts the hours or days on which they are prepared to work unless they can show that there is a reasonable prospect of getting such a job. In theory, therefore, someone who is made redundant from a regular two days a week job, and who does not wish to work longer hours, should be able to claim benefit for two days a week (provided there is a reasonable supply of similar part-time jobs locally). But benefit can be withdrawn if a claimant turns down any 'reasonable' job, provided that it offers at least 24 hours a week! In other words, somebody who wants to work part-time for less than 24 hours a week can be forced – through the withdrawal of benefit – to accept a job with longer hours; and somebody who wants to work full-time, for more than 30 hours, can be forced to accept a job with shorter hours.

To make matters worse, different rules apply to means-tested income support, which can be claimed where unemployment benefit is inadequate or has run out. An income support claimant (other than a lone parent) also needs to show that they are available for work: but this time, they must be available for at least 24 hours a week. As with unemployment benefit, refusal of a job which offers at least those hours can lead to a reduction of benefit.

Since April 1992, however, a different rule – a 16-hours threshold – applies to someone receiving income support who manages to get a part-time job. A lone parent can now only qualify for income support as long as her part-time work is below 16 hours (and her income is below the income support limits). Once she crosses the hours threshold, she is debarred from income support and must instead claim means-tested family credit if her earnings are too low to support herself and her children. This change in the rules was designed, together with changes in maintenance regulations, to free lone parents from income support and enable them to rely on earnings, maintenance, child benefit and (if necessary) family credit instead.[37] At the same time, however, the income support regulations no longer allow a lone parent to deduct her child care expenses from her part-time earnings before benefit starts to be reduced – a measure which can act as a real disincentive against part-time employment.

The 16-hour rule also applies to childless single claimants and to couples. Thus, a single person who takes a job of 16 hours or more will no longer be entitled to income support, however low their earnings; nor will they be able to claim family credit, which is only available to those with children. A similar disincentive to work more than 16 hours a week or more also now affects the partner of an unemployed claimant. For instance, a married man who loses his full-time job will be debarred from income support if his wife works above this threshold. Although she will be entitled to claim family credit if her earnings are low, the family will lose the assistance with mortgage interest payments and the free school meals which come with income support but not with family credit.

An already complicated system has been made even more so by this new 16-hours threshold for income support claimants, which is consistent with employment protection law, but inconsistent with other income support and unemployment benefit regulations. Furthermore, a change designed to encourage lone parents to take part-time work will *discourage* single claimants and the wives of unemployed men from doing so.

The basis of reform

In order to make sense of this muddle, we have to distinguish between two different situations.

First, there is the person who wants to work full-time, who is available to work full-time, but who can only find a part-time job while continuing to seek additional work. Someone in this position should also be able to claim part-time unemployment benefit, to compensate for the shortfall in hours worked. In Sweden, Denmark, Belgium and the Netherlands, the unemployment benefit system offers a *pro rata* benefit of just this kind. Although it would be consistent in principle and simple in practice to pay part-time unemployment benefit regardless of the level of part-time earnings, it would seem fair to taper off benefit after part-time earnings went above a certain level in order to avoid a situation where someone able to earn the equivalent of a full-time salary on part-time hours could also obtain partial unemployment benefit.

Second, there is the person who wants to work part-time, who is only available to work part-time – and who should, if unemployed, be able to claim part-time unemployment benefit. In order that benefits can be calculated on a *pro rata* basis, the social security system will need to define a 'standard working week'. By replacing the loss of part-time earnings, the unemployment benefit system would recognise that part-time earnings are as important to the part-time employee as full-time earnings are to the full-timer.

The possible structure of a part-time benefit, based on a notional standard week of 30 hours, is explained in detail by Lynda Bransbury.[38] But there is a further question to be considered. If the part-time worker is only available for part-time work because of her family responsibilities, should the benefit system also compensate her for the earnings sacrificed by her work at home? For example, should a mother who divides her time between paid employment and looking after her children be able to claim a part-time benefit in addition to her earnings?

Under the present system, a lone parent does not have to establish her availability for work in order to claim income support. As we have seen, the government has recently changed the rules in order to float many lone parents off income support and on to a combination of part-time employment, maintenance and means-tested family credit. An alternative approach would be to allow a lone parent with a part-time job to claim a part-time benefit to compensate her for the hours when she was not available for employment. As with part-time unemployment benefit, some limit would also need to be set on the level of part-time earnings before benefit was reduced. But such an approach could be more generous, providing lower marginal tax rates, than the government's reliance on means-tested family credit to supplement a lone parent's part-time earnings.

In the case of a married couple, or those living together as man and wife, only one partner – usually, but not necessarily, the man – can claim income support and the couple's income is added together for the calculation of benefit. It would be possible to allow a parent within a couple, who is working part-time in order to care for children, to claim a part-time benefit in her own right. But if the part-time employee can claim a part-time caring benefit, then presumably the full-time mother should be able to claim a full-time caring benefit too (just as the lone mother without any employment can claim income support). In either case, this individual approach to benefits for a married or cohabiting parent runs up against the problem that while it would benefit women in households where the man's income is not fully shared with his family, it would create obvious unfairness where the other partner had a good income which was fully shared in the household. Furthermore, as Ruth Lister has stressed,[39] making it easier for women to achieve an independent income through social security may not only reinforce the division of work between women and men but make it *more* difficult for women to achieve independence through paid employment.

As far as benefits are concerned, the priority is to establish a part-time benefit to cover the two clear cases of the part-time worker who loses her job, and the full-time worker who can only obtain a part-time job. At the same time, the calculation of hours normally worked, and the qualifications for benefit, need to be reformed to take account of various forms of non-standard employment. These changes would go a long way towards integrating part-time employment within both the social security system and the labour market.

Flexible working and retirement

As we saw earlier, part-time employees often miss out on the occupational pension schemes which, increasingly, make the difference between poverty and comfort in retirement and old age. The equal treatment principle would require employers to open up occupational schemes to part-time workers, or to provide contributions to personal pension schemes, on a *pro rata* basis.

Part-time employees and others whose employment does not fit the standard full-time pattern may also lose out on state pensions. Someone whose earnings are below the national insurance contributions limit for more than a brief period will only qualify for a reduced flat-rate retirement pension at the age of 60. Similarly, irregular patterns of work over several years can make it impossible to meet contribution conditions. The proposed reform of contributions, crediting in employees with earnings below the limit, and extending protection to all employees who work at least eight hours a week on average would be of real benefit to part-time workers.

For many parents, the state earnings related pension scheme (SERPS) provides far more effective protection than an occupational scheme or a personal pension can hope to do. Initially providing pensions based on an individual's twenty best years' earnings, SERPS offered a route to security in retirement which would not be affected by several years' spent at home or in low-paid, possibly part-time work. For those retiring after 1999, however, the SERPS pension will, like the national insurance pension, be based on contributions paid during a 'full working life' (from 16 to the pension age, with up to five years ignored).

The impact of this change is, however, somewhat softened by the provision for 'home responsibilities protection' for up to 20 years. Any year spent caring for a child or an elderly dependant is protected, provided that the carer is receiving either child benefit or invalid care allowance. The restrictions on receipt of invalid care allowance, however, mean that protection will be denied to some carers who need it.[40] More fundamentally, home responsibilities protection is only available for complete years and thus, once again, ignores the realities of flexible labour.

Take the example of a woman who spends five years at home looking after children fulltime, followed by ten years combining part-time employment with the care of children and an elderly mother. With home responsibilities protection, the first five years will be ignored when her 'working life' is calculated for her pension entitlements. But her protection is lost during the following ten years, with the result that her low part-time earnings depress the level of her SERPS pension. From the point of view of her pension, she would have been better off having those years ignored completely, so that her pension could be calculated on the basis of full-time employment before and after her caring years. Rather than penalise part-time employment in this way, the 'twenty best years' rule should be reinstated or home responsibilities protection extended to part-years as well as full.

Life begins at forty?

The model of a standard working lifetime brings with it powerful stereotypes of what people can and cannot do at different ages. While the notion of 'age appropriate behaviour' may be useful and appropriate to child development, it is increasingly inappropriate and restrictive when applied to adults. Stereotypes based on a male working lifetime are particularly inhibiting when they are applied to women.

It is, for instance, widely assumed that only younger people can provide the energy, dynamism and willingness to travel and work all hours required in a wide range of marketing, management and other jobs. For many female jobs, particularly secretarial, a hidden requirement is personal attractiveness which, again, is taken to imply youth. Hence the age bars which are routinely found in job advertisements.

Behind these age bars lie the usual assumptions about men's and women's work. Just at the time they are becoming fathers, younger men will be available to work the hours which make family life virtually impossible – because women will be available to care for the children. The result is to divide men from their children and women from their careers. And because women remain more likely to take a break from employment, or to move from full-time to part-time work, age bars are almost inevitably sex discriminatory. The 'career age' of a woman who has spent several years partly or wholly caring for children at home is very different from her chronological age. One of the first successful challenges to indirect sex discrimination under the 1975 Sex Discrimination Act established precisely this point, forcing the Civil Service to raise substantially the age-limit of 35 which they had previously imposed.[41]

Already, we are seeing in industrialised countries the emergence of a wide variety of *different* working lifetimes as individuals respond in different ways to social and economic pressures and opportunities. This is, for instance, the first generation where one 40-year-old woman whose children are leaving school can be working alongside a colleague of the same age who is starting her family, needing paid maternity leave and considering more flexible hours. The woman – and the man – who postpone their parenting may well be available for long hours and unpredictable travel in their 20s and 30s: but those who have their children young may equally relish the challenge of new and demanding employment in their 40s and 50s.

It is unlawful in Britain to bar women or people from ethnic minority communities from entire categories of employment. As Alan Walker and Tom Schuller have argued, it is high time to outlaw age discrimination as well.[42] The USA, for example, has had an Age Discrimination in Employment Act since 1967, making compulsory retirement unlawful on grounds of age alone for federal employees of any age. Other employers may not compulsorily retire workers on age grounds alone under the age of 70. As a first step, employment protection laws should be extended to people up to that age. More fundamentally, the opportunity should be taken of a reform of existing sex and race discrimination laws to remove age bars in recruitment, training and promotion except where there is an overwhelming reason for their retention.

Flexible retirement

More flexible working hours and working lives demand more flexible retirement. Compulsory retirement at 60 or 65 is out-of-date in a society where a woman of 60 can expect to live a further 21 years – about the same as the life-expectancy of a man of 50 at the beginning of this century.[43] It also ignores the large and growing disparities in health and income amongst people over the age of 60. Those whose incomes are low – often because of low-paid, insecure and part-time employment earlier in their lives – may need to continue working to supplement an inadequate pension. Those whose health is poor (often those with low incomes as well), or who have suffered industrial injuries, have no choice but to retire and must be able to do so on a decent income. Among the growing number of better-off older people – who have paid off their mortgage and have good occupational pensions – some will want to continue employment which they find challenging and enjoyable. As we saw in chapter 4, many people in their 50s and 60s would prefer part-time employment to full-time retirement.

To encompass such a range of individual needs, two fundamental changes are needed: first, the option of part-time retirement; and second, a choice of when to retire.

Earlier, I proposed a part-time unemployment benefit. Following the example of Sweden, which has operated a partial pension scheme since 1976, we now need to offer a part-time pension to those who want to continue working part-time. Alan Walker, in the study I referred to earlier, has described a scheme which would allow people working under 16 hours a week to claim a full pension and those working between 16 and 30 hours to claim a partial pension, *pro rata* to the hours worked. Because the national insurance retirement pension has been 'earned' by contributions paid during the working life, and is paid regarless of other income, the level of part-time earnings should not affect the level of the part-pension.

The second reform concerns the pension age itself. Britain's discriminatory pension ages have been challenged by the European Community. Occupational pension schemes have been required to harmonise their pension age and the government has promised reform of state pension ages.

To simplify a highly technical issue, the problem is that reducing men's pension age to 60 would cost the taxpayer a substantial sum; increasing women's pension age to 65 (or harmonising at, say, 63) would cost women a substantial sum, by forcing them to work longer to earn the same pension or to take a reduced pension in order to retire at the same age as before.

The sensible way forward is to introduce a flexible 'decade of retirement', allowing men and women to choose between the ages of 60 and 70 when to take full or part retirement. At the upper age, the full pension would be paid regardless of any hours worked, while within the decade someone continuing to work should have the option of paying additional contributions to earn an additional pension – a flexibility which could be particularly valuable to those with an interrupted working life.

The changes which I have outlined may seem daunting. As I have indicated, it would be unreasonable to expect them to be introduced simultaneously. But the extent of the changes needed is itself a perfect illustration of how far the model of a standard working life underlies public policy, inhibiting the new kinds of flexibility which are increasingly demanded by individuals and by enterprise.

7 THE CHALLENGE TO MANAGERS

Law reform can provide both a level playing field for different working time contracts and a boundary fence of health and safety requirements. But it is the policies and strategies adopted within each organisation which will have the most profound effect on the way we work in future.

Employers in Britain and other European countries have already gone a long way towards initiating or accepting part-time and other non-standard working time arrangements. In doing so, they have achieved substantial economic benefits.

In some cases, flexible working time arrangements have been achieved at the expense of employees. But in general, the problem is not that employers have gone too far: the problem is that they have not gone far enough.

I have already argued (see above, p.88) why it is in the interests of employers as well as employees to integrate part-timers within the workforce and, in particular, to give them a legal right to the same terms and conditions of employment, on a *pro rata* basis, as full-timers. Here I turn to a more diffuse and deep-seated problem: the 'working time culture' of companies and other organisations.

Working all hours

In most occupations, success depends on working long hours, year in, year out. For manual employees, high – or even adequate – earnings have traditionally depended on long basic and overtime hours. For white-collar workers seeking promotion to a management position or aiming to do well in a profession, even a long formal working day and week may not be enough: they are also likely to be judged on whether or not they are willing to work all hours, to put their job first. Effective working hours may include socialising in the pub 'after work', taking work home in the evenings and at weekends, getting to work early in the morning.

A MORI survey in 1992 of 200 British directors and senior managers found that almost half were at their desks by 8 a.m. and about a quarter still there after 6.30 p.m. More than two-thirds worked at least one weekend a month and fewer than half took their full holidays. Not surprisingly, they were 'over-worked, stressed and found it difficult to combine a career with family life.'[1]

Britain's own legislators traditionally work a bizarre working day, with the House of Commons sitting from 2.30 p.m. to 10.30 p.m. Monday to Thursday, with a morning sitting on Friday. In practice, the hours are usually longer, with about two in three 'days' continuing after 10.30 p.m. and one in three lasting until after midnight. Devised to meet the needs of men who generally combined their Parliamentary duties with another career at the Bar or elsewhere, the system has more recently been defended on the grounds that it leaves the morning clear for Ministerial business and the work of Parliamentary Committees. Not surprisingly, it has been condemned for deterring women from seeking entry to Parliament, exiling male MPs from their own families and lowering the quality of Parliamentary work.[2] Reforms have now been promised, which would trade late-night sittings for more morning work.

The pattern varies from organisation to organisation. But the underlying assumption is the same: someone who wants to get on either has no other responsibilities or, more probably, has a wife to take care of them.

Advancement also depends on a life-time, as well as a daily or weekly, working pattern. Again, the specific pattern varies between organisations and occupations: swimmers peak before the age of 20, judges do not retire until their 70s. But in most, there is a clear notion of what is 'too young' and what is 'too old'.

Academic careers offer just one illustration of the problem. Between 1988 and 1990, Andrea Spurling carried out a detailed study of the careers of women university teachers, based on King's College, Cambridge, which had been admitting women as students and Fellows for nearly two decades. Higher education generally, and Cambridge in particular, has very few women in senior positions. As Spurling found:

> the profession expects proof through publications, lectures and attendance at conferences of a history of continuous attention to academic research. Women and men who had combined academic work with practical domestic responsibility felt their efficiency in each area had been seriously compromised. . . . The areas of conflict most frequently highlighted include, for a woman, establishing an academic career and a family in the 25 to 35 age decade.[3]

A similar conflict between biological and career clocks is found in medicine, where women are only 15% of consultants and only 1% of consultant general surgeons. Extremely long hours for junior doctors (see above, p.86) are compounded by what one writer described as 'the age-stage link in the rigid medical career structure which hits training surgeons hardest in their late 20s to mid 30s. This is when you must get on to the next two rungs of the ladder – senior registrar or consultant – which frequently defeat women.' Wendy Love, a consultant surgeon in obstetrics and gynaecology, argues that 'if you miss a rung, it's hard to get back on. If you take a few years out for a family, you will never be a surgeon.' The few women who have succeeded in becoming both consultants and mothers generally postponed starting a family until they had already become consultants.[4] Dr Ruth Gilbert, a member of the BMA's junior staff committee, has urged an expansion of part-time training, with 'part-time jobs which are part of the mainstream, not add-ons. All clinical medical work is carried out on a sessional basis, so why shouldn't doctors working up to 40 and 80 hours a week work alongside each other?'[5]

Men will earn, women will care

In other words, the working time expectations with which most of us are familiar reflect the old male model of continuous, full-time, life-time employment and the old assumption that men will earn and women will care.

The impact of this collision between the old assumptions and the new workforce is largely felt by the women who juggle the conflicting demands of career and caring. Either they slip down the occupational ladder into part-time jobs or they suffer the stress of trying to compete 'on equal terms' with men. If they take a break from full-time employment, then they are 'too old' at 40 or 50 to be promoted or, in some cases, even appointed to well-paid and responsible work.

We come back here to the question of equal opportunities. It is not surprising that anti-discrimination laws and the adoption of equal opportunities policies by management have had on the whole disappointing results. If work and family cannot be fitted together reasonably smoothly, then as things stand it is women rather than men whose employment will be affected. But if women are unable to combine their family responsibilities with employment that makes full use of their abilities and training, it is *employers*, as well as the women themselves, who lose out.

Commercial and organisational success requires equal opportunities policies that work. Equal opportunities require a new approach to the relationship between work and family. And that, in turn, means re-organising working time.

These links are beginning to be made by top management. TSB Bank, for instance, announced in 1991 that it had replaced the previous 29 weeks' maternity leave with a new entitlement for mothers and fathers (including adoptive parents) to one year's parental leave, and extended its career break scheme to people caring for elderly, sick and disabled dependants. The company's objectives included improving retention rates among staff with family responsibilities.[6]

The Opportunity 2000 initiative, launched by Business in the Community in 1991, published a summary of the equality goals and strategies of several leading companies. Although many did not specify how they believed they could reach their aim of increasing the proportion of women in senior jobs, it is also striking that many referred to flexible working time arrangements.

In some cases, these were only seen to affect women: for instance, the merchant bank, Henry Ansbacher, referred to 'further flexible working arrangements for women who need to balance the demands of their work with family commitments,' while Boots planned 'to improve the flexibility of working conditions to meet the needs of female staff'. Others referred to the need to move flexible working arrangements up the ladder: both Midland and National Westminster planned to make flexible working available in management posts and Safeway referred to women already working in part-time management. And a few, like Avon Cosmetics, specifically mentioned the need to promote flexible working and career breaks 'for men and women'.[7]

As we have seen in this report, many organisations have begun to make special provision for women's different time needs. But almost none has fundamentally questioned their working time culture or tried to create a new pattern at every level of their operation.

The five lives of a workplace

As we consider the different attitudes of employers towards different groups of employees – manual and non-manual, women and men, full-time and part-time – we can identify five 'lives' in the development of organisations, five stages of working time reform.

Of course, real organisations present a more complicated picture. But this scheme is designed to help both managers and employees analyse and develop their own strategies.

Stage one: the segregated firm

Part-timers are employed, possibly in large numbers. But occupations remain rigidly segregated – there are part-time jobs and full-time jobs. Most or all of the part-time employees are women. Most or all of the part-time jobs are low paid, low status and low in (acknowledged) skill. Part-time employees receive lower hourly rates of pay than full-timers in comparable jobs and are excluded from the firm's pension scheme, training, promotion arrangements and so on.

There are similarly rigid divisions between white-collar and blue-collar employees. Senior managers have considerable working time autonomy – although, of course, they all work full-time – while manual and clerical staff must clock on and off.

Maternity leave arrangements are the statutory minimum, for full-timers as well as part-timers. There is a compulsory retirement age.

Stage two: separate but equal

Part-time jobs are still segregated but their importance to the organisation is acknowledged. Part-timers have the same terms and conditons, *pro rata*, as full-timers. They are entitled to join the company's pension scheme.

In the industrial sector, new shift patterns have enabled average weekly hours for manual full-time employees to be cut. Those nearing retirement age are given some time off in the months before retirement. There are some employees over retirement age to meet labour shortages.

Stage three: half-way there

Flexible working time has moved up the occupational ladder. Job-sharing is permitted within a range of white-collar jobs. Career breaks have been introduced for management posts. Maternity leave arrangements are better than the statutory minimum. Flexible working time, however, is a response to the needs of women. Paternity leave, if it exists, is brief and not encouraged. The development of part-time careers is still hindered by the persistence of the full-time, male career pattern.

Shift patterns for manual employees may accommodate part-time workers as well (working, for instance, half the hours of a full-time shift worker). Conditions for manual and non-manual employees have been harmonised.

Stage four: the innovative firm

A wide variety of working time contracts are in operation, in both manual and non-manual jobs. Depending on the nature of the organisation, they include annual hours contracts, term-time working and individual choice of working hours. Special leave is available – for instance, for people with families abroad; or to meet a need for retraining.

Those nearing retirement age are enabled to reduce their working hours for several months before retirement. The employment of workers over retirement age is encouraged.

Stage five: the new workplace

The organisation has created a new working time culture. There are no longer 'part-time' and 'full-time' jobs. Instead, most people – including some at a senior level – have personalised working time arrangements, chosen from a variety of options.

The organisation has thought out its strategy for improving the relationship between work and family, and paternity leave is not only permitted but encouraged. Working shorter hours is no longer confined to women with young children: shorter hours workers include those nearing or over 'retirement age' and those with responsibility for elderly dependants. Retirement itself is flexible; compulsory retirement at a fixed age has been abolished.

Making flexibility work

In the mid-1980s, John Atkinson of the Institute of Manpower Studies developed the model of the 'flexible firm', which treats part-time, temporary and sub-contracted workers as part of the flexible 'periphery' in contrast to the 'core' of permanent employees.[8] Despite criticisms, the model has been widely influential in labour market analysis. But part-time employees and others working on non-standard contracts are not necessarily 'peripheral' employees; instead, they are increasingly regarded by employers as part of their permanent workforce. One aim of public policy should be to reinforce and encourage this development. Instead of a single model which treats non-standard working time arrangements as 'peripheral', we need a more flexible analysis of flexibility itself.

Most organisations have adopted part-time or other non-standard forms of employment: now they need to rethink the division between full-time and part-time employment. Many have reduced the hours of full-timers: now they need to challenge the assumption that most jobs can *only* be done full-time and actively create opportunities for shorter hours working.

Other studies confirm that the most successful working time innovations have taken place in companies which have adopted new arrangements as part of a long-term business strategy for improving competitiveness. In the case of the British car firm, Rover, for instance, radical shift changes to permit continuous working are only one element in an attempt to transform the organisation's culture through employee self-development schemes, flexible skills, quality action teams and enhanced job security. The motive? An urgent need to compete with Japanese firms.[9]

The IPM study comments that, in the industrial sector:

> a great influence on such strategies is the generally held belief that basic working hours are almost certain at some time to decline yet further . . . [either] as a result of negotiations [or] as a result of their own harmonization policies, which are themselves the almost inevitable result of new technologies and the blurring of staff/manual demarcation lines.[10]

Developing workplace policies

It is surprising how many organisations simply do not know what proportion of their workforce work less than full-time hours and what the range of part-time hours are. But without this basic information, managers cannot begin to assess what they are losing in productivity and potential.

An organisation looking to improve its performance through working time reform should, therefore, conduct a Working Time Audit. This will establish how far the company has already adopted non-standard working time arrangements. More important, it will help managers analyse how further flexibility could help them, for instance, match output to demand, use the existing workforce more productively, and improve recruitment and retention rates.

The next stage is to develop a Work and Family Policy, designed to improve the organisation's performance by making it easier for employees to combine their work with their family.

Detailed advice is available to companies wanting to develop packages for employees caring for children and other dependants, or to make the best use of specific non-standard employment arrangements.[11] But less advice is available about how to integrate working time changes into a comprehensive work-family policy. Many of the working time arrangements I have described earlier should provide inspiration; some of the specific steps which could be taken are described below.

Policies for shorter working hours

First, every job within the organisation should be assessed to see if it is appropriate for shorter hours working (including job-sharing by two part-timers). Some senior management jobs may not lend themselves to part-time work, for instance if they require continuous and consistent contact with other staff. Some work requires a continuous presence during set hours, for instance lawyers appearing in court. But managers and trades unionists may be surprised by what happens if they have to justify the requirement to work full-time, year-round.

As part of this review of shorter hours working, there is a need to integrate part-time working into the organisation's career path. As a first step, those employed in part-time jobs should be offered opportunities for training and promotion into more demanding and rewarding work. But the aim should be to make it possible for someone moving towards a senior management post to progress via a period of part-time employment – or even to be appointed to a senior, part-time management post.

Second, any vacancy to be filled should be opened to job-sharers unless there are over-riding reasons why two people could not share that particular job.

Third, organisations should consider the adoption of a 'voluntary shorter hours' arrangement similar to that accepted by the Inland Revenue (see above, p.31). Priority should be given to parents of young children and to those approaching retirement; but there is no reason why opportunities for shorter hours working should not be made more widely available where they are compatible with the organisation of the work.

Individual working hours contracts

Depending on the nature of the work involved, individual hours contracts (see above, p.46) may offer a way of combining maximum choice for employees with an effective matching of output and demand. They have particular advantages from the point of view of a work/family policy which is trying to break down male stereotypes about working hours.

The challenge with any move to more individual choice of working hours is to match employees' preferences to the enterprise's needs. Payment systems have an obvious role to play. In the case of the West German department store quoted on p.46, commissions helped to ensure that more staff worked on the days and at the hours when there were more customers.

A large organisation could consider a variation on the theme of personalised hours, which builds on traditional shift systems. Within each job category, managers would establish the combination of different working time contracts needed for efficient operation. Each employee would then be offered a choice of 'shifts'. First choice of working time arrangements could be offered to, say, lone parents; second choice to others with dependent children; third choice to people with other dependent relatives, and so on. The least popular hours would attract a special premium, compensating those in the lowest priority category who had little or no choice. Employees and their unions could themselves help determine what priority should be given to different groups, as well as the premium to be paid for 'anti-social hours working'.

Although the prospect of a large number of employees working different hours may horrify managers used to traditional arrangements, computerisation of personnel and work records makes such flexibility not only possible but efficient.

Career breaks

Unless the work itself demands almost continuous training and experience (as in information technology, for instance), organisations should also consider the possibility of introducing unpaid 'career breaks'. These can form an important part of a work/family policy (as they do already in many financial institutions), but they need not be restricted in this way.

From the employer's point of view, an unpaid career break is equivalent to special unpaid leave, although the two are usually treated as different. A single policy could allow employees to apply for a specified period of unpaid leave, with priority given to people with family responsibilities, followed perhaps by those wishing to pursue education and training, and those wanting to visit families abroad. Any policy for career breaks should, of course, include appropriate refresher training on the employee's return and may also provide for the employee to keep in touch during the period of the break.

Age bars

Shorter hours working needs to be integrated within an organisation's career path. But promotion opportunities may also be needlessly blocked by unjustified requirements or expectations about age. As we saw in the last chapter (see p.135 above), age bars on appointment or promotion are usually a form of indirect sex discrimination and have been successfully challenged under the Sex Discrimination Act. Even more important from the manager's point of view than the risk of a legal action is the likelihood that good candidates are being ruled out. An organisation should, therefore, spell out the age bars which it imposes on recruitment and promotion and consider whether they are really necessary.

Time banks: a new role for pension schemes

Britain has a large industry of state, occupational and personal pension schemes designed to enable people to redistribute income from the time they spend in employment to the time they spend in retirement.

It is now time to take a new step forward and turn pension schemes into 'time banks' which would enable people to redistribute their time and money *before* they retire as well as after. Today, few people other than academics can enjoy sabbatical leave from their employment. But there is no reason why everybody who is willing and able to save some of their earnings at one period in their lives should not be able to enjoy paid time off at another. Just like retirement, paid time off could be used to spend more time with children and family. It could be devoted to education, study and travel or simply enjoyed as 'free' time.

To take an example: a 21-year-old decides to save one week's earnings a year in a 'time bank'. As with existing pension schemes, contributions attract tax relief, as do investments made by the fund. By the age of 32, he has accumulated thirteen weeks' paid leave, of which he takes seven to spend at home after his first baby is born. He makes no further contributions for three years, and then starts saving a week a year again. By the age of 44 he is entitled to sixteen weeks' leave, which he uses to attend a short business management course before setting up a small business of his own.[12]

A scheme of this kind – which also allowed its members to 'borrow' paid leave out of future earnings – was proposed by the Norwegian Commission on Working Hours in 1987. In its 'report from the year 2,000', imagining the effects of the scheme (which has not yet been introduced), the Commission described a nationwide system of computer terminals in local welfare offices, allowing members of the voluntary leave fund to gain immediate information on the state of their 'leave account,' as well as their pension points.

The Commission suggested that the leave fund would 'reduce the problem concerning the discrepancy during one's life-span between earnings and expenses'. Young people setting up a new home would be able to convert accumulated leave points into cash, or to use the fund to compensate for reduced hours of work because of child care. But because no security was required from people borrowing out of the fund, the Commission envisaged that some fund members would leave the country permanently with an overdraft in their account![13]

More recently, the chairman of the Parliamentary Select Committee on Social Security, Frank Field MP, has also suggested that individuals should be entitled to regular statements of their national insurance contribution accounts, and given greater rights to use their occupational or pension scheme entitlements before as well as after retirement. The British government or the Select Committee should now examine what changes to pension legislation would be required. Obviously, the individual's right to return to work after paid leave should also be safeguarded.

If time savings schemes of this kind became popular, there would need to be rules about the number of employees in one company who could take extended leave at the same time. But imaginative employers could find that just as career breaks can help attract and retain skilled women employees, 'time banks' would help in the increasingly intense competition for high-quality workers.

The challenge to management

Managers who are used to managing full-time workforces on standard hours may throw up their hands in horror at the complications of trying to manage people working a wide variety of hours in a wide variety of jobs. There are certainly costs involved, including the need to retrain managers in a new approach to the organisation of working time and the balance between work and family. But information technology offers new opportunities to manage a complex variety of working time contracts in highly efficient ways.

As most of the companies referred to earlier found, careful planning and consultation with employees is essential if substantial changes to working hours are to be successful. In some cases, limits need to be set for the proportions of people working full-time and those working part-time, term-time or other shorter hours arrangements, in order to ensure that full-time staff are not left filling in unpopular times or unable themselves to take holidays during school holidays.

Although small organisations are often highly flexible, it may be difficult where there is only one person filling a particular responsibility in a small company or unit to enable him or her to move to shorter hours. As the EOC employees' survey found, however, there is significant evidence of 'a high level of trust and co-operation between employer and employee,' with a real willingness on the part of many managers and employees to trade flexibility to mutual advantage.[14] Such informal arrangements are likely to remain as important as formal policies in making the most of flexibility.

The Civil Service itself offers an example of how managers can respond to the challenge. Although each government department and Next Steps agency is responsible for its own personnel management, the Office of the Minister for the Civil Service and the Treasury have taken steps to stress the benefits to managers of flexible working hours – benefits which include a greater ability to attract and retain the best staff, reduced absenteeism and higher productivity, and a more efficient match between workforce and workload.

In many organisations, there will be prejudices about part-time: part-time work is 'only for women', part-timers can't be flexible/work weekends/work late in a crisis, a part-timer can't work to top management (let alone become top management), somebody working part-time doesn't really want the extra burdens of promotion. These and other myths are dispelled as more managers actually take responsibility for managing part-time employees – and, better still, as more managers themselves work part-time. But positive steps can also be taken to counter prejudice. A Civil Service training video on equal opportunities, for example, includes an imaginary case-study of a part-time employee with an excellent performance appraisal, whose manager failed to recommend her for promotion on the grounds that 'she wouldn't want the extra hassle and anyway she'd never be able to do overnight trips.'

Sticking to the old ways will make life easier for managers. But it will deprive them of the chance to make their organisations more efficient and to get the best out of their employees – women as well as men. The costs of change are real: but the costs of refusing to change are greater.

8 THE CHALLENGE TO TRADE UNIONS

The trade union movement has often been suspicious of working time flexibility, seeing it as part of a process of work intensification, cost-cutting and reduction of job security. Until recently, few unions had undertaken any detailed analysis of innovative working time arrangements; one union-sponsored study concluded that unions find it 'hard to think in terms other than a weekly wage for a defined working week on the basis of an eight hour day'.[1]

Trades unions' attitudes have been heavily influenced by the association in Britain of working time flexibility with labour market deregulation. The Conservative government's support for part-time employment increased fears that part-time employees would be used to undermine the wages and working conditions of full-timers and to reduce the availability of secure full-time employment. Earlier union hostility to part-time employment has, however, given way to a new emphasis on equal rights for part-time with full-time employees.

Several different factors including the outcome of negotiations and disputes over many decades help to shape each union's response to working time questions. Because unions exist to defend their members' interests, policy will reflect the composition and attitudes of existing members. But a union seeking to recruit amongst part-time or temporary workers, or wanting to give a proper emphasis to the needs of women, may find tensions between the needs of different groups of actual or future members. A manufacturing union with a strong tradition of collectively negotiated hours will also have a very different approach from a service or general union where non-standard working time arrangements may be more common.

In this chapter, I look at three aspects of unions' policies: the campaign for a shorter working week; attitudes to part-time employees and more generally to non-standard working time contracts; and the conflict between individualised and collectively determined working hours.

Winning a shorter working week

The main focus of trade union concern about working time has been the shorter working week for full-time employees, particularly manual workers in industry. At the beginning of chapter 2, I described the successful campaign by the Confederation of Shipbuilding and Engineering Unions for a cut of two hours in the engineering industry's working week.

This campaign succeeded primarily because it reflected the strongly-held working time preferences of unions' own members. It involved a significant change to the working week – an extra half-day on the weekend – rather than a few minutes off the working day. Campaign literature stressed the benefits to both women and men of the extra time for families, domestic responsibilities and leisure. For instance, one AEU campaign leaflet illustrated the man who used his Friday afternoon to fetch his children from school *and* go fishing – an example which may have seemed a little optimistic to women!

Throughout the industry, shorter hours were usually paid for by productivity gains. For instance, the agreement between British Aerospace at Chester and the manual employees' unions stated that: 'The company and trade unions agree that any reduction in working hours must not increase costs or reduce business efficiency and productivity. Therefore the company and trade unions agree that a shorter working week is possible through agreed improvements in productivity and changes to previous working practices.' Similar commitments are to be found in other 37-hour agreements, including that with Rolls Royce.

Many of the agreements also contained commitments to cut absenteeism and measures to reduce tea breaks. And shorter working hours were often linked to flexibility in job content – with reductions in demarcation between different crafts, acceptance of training for multi-skilling and commitments to improved quality and productivity. In some cases, as we have seen, the 37-hour week was also accompanied by a move to continuous production.

How flexible is flexible?

Manufacturing trades unions operate within a context of standard working hours which are usually determined collectively. Shift systems may involve substantial variation from week to week or month to month, in the arrangement and total of hours worked by each individual. But they are based on uniform hours for each shift of production workers, rostered over a period of several months – not on the wide variety of individual working hours contracts which are increasingly to be found in service employment.

In general, the issue for manufacturing unions is not to defend the *uniformity* of their members' hours, but to achieve a cut in hours without a reduction in pay or a worsening of other conditions. Nonetheless, the trade-off between shorter working hours and increased productivity may in practice challenge trade union assumptions about normal or acceptable working hours. A nine-hour-day/four-day week or weekend-only jobs clearly threaten long-established goals.

The starting-point must be the preferences of union members themselves. A union which fails to reflect those preferences may lose members or simply fail to recruit them: worse still, a union which opposes a working time proposal that is popular with its members risks being bypassed in a deal done directly between employer and employees.

The Confederation campaign stressed the importance of the working week, rather than the working day. Other union agreements (see chapter 2 for examples) have been based on a fortnight, a month or even longer. Thus, in deciding how to respond to employers' working time proposals – or what changes to initiate itself – a union needs to consider the overall effect of the change.

The eight-hour day, for instance, was a central union demand in a time of uniform working days and working weeks. But it is too often forgotten that the campaign for an eight-hour day was achieved at a time of a six-day working week. Today, a 48-hour week is unacceptably long to most workers (although worked by many). The eight-hour day need not be regarded as sacrosanct if the working week itself is acceptably short. A working week of four nine-hour or even ten-hour days is popular with many employees: it should not be opposed by unions simply because it breaches the eight-hour day. Many existing agreements, of course, involve even longer working shifts. Such arrangements require, however, proper arrangements to protect health and safety, since a longer day will have very different effects in different jobs and industries.

As I indicated earlier, unions have begun to agree deals which breach the eight-hour day but produce dramatic reductions in the average working week. Defending the eight-hour day (which is routinely breached by overtime in any case) may be appropriate in some cases: it is unlikely to be effective as a general strategy. Instead, the eight-hour day – and other standard working time arrangements – are likely to become bargaining counters in negotiations with employers to reduce working time in other directions.

Increasingly, industrial trades unions will need to decide what they regard as the *outside* limit for the working day or shift – a twelve-hour shift three times within a week? an eleven-hour shift twice within a week? and so on – and then negotiate within these limits for shorter average working weeks combined with longer blocks of time off.

Similarly, a six-day week may be acceptable if it alternates with a four-day week, if employees decide that a three-day weekend each fortnight compensates for the disruption of social and family life involved in the alternating one-day weekend. Acceptability may be strengthened if productivity gains are available to pay for improved wages and/or avoid redundancies.

Proposals for annual hours contracts need to be approached in a similar spirit. Depending on the kind of work involved, a permanent workforce engaged in long weeks in high season and short weeks in low season, with earnings evenly spread throughout the year, may be preferable to the use of temporary workers and/or long overtime in high season (see p.42 for examples). Attention to health and safety is vital, since a danger with such contracts is that they may involve several weeks or months of long daily and weekly hours. And unions may also need to negotiate 'plus payments', to compensate for the withdrawal of overtime and anti-social hours premia as a result of the move to annual hours contracts.

Shift arrangements which defy both the eight-hour day and the five-day week, and annual hours contracts which mean a longer working week for part of the year, can have real disadvantages for employees. But they can also be the most effective way of delivering substantial cuts in working hours – and delivering them, furthermore, in the longer blocks of time off which workers are most likely to prefer.

The six-day week in coal-mining

Questions like this have proved particularly controversial within the coal-mining industry. For several years, British Coal has been considering the possibility of six-day working, permitting a more intensive use of capital equipment. So far, only the new mine at Asfordby operates six days a week. For individuals, the five-day week has been replaced by three weeks of six days followed by one week off. Shifts are longer than before, but total hours over the year remain the same. Pay has been increased to compensate for weekend working. British Coal believe that 'the revised working pattern – particularly the rostered-off week – is welcomed by the majority of mineworkers. . . . the arrangements allow more intensive working of the colliery, whilst the individual's annual hours are broadly the same and additional pay is earned.'[2]

The National Union of Mineworkers (NUM) takes a very different view. A paper presented to the NUM Conference in 1987 condemned the 'political offensive over six day working' as a continuation of British Coal's long-standing campaign to close pits and shed jobs. There is no disagreement about the productivity gains from a six-day week: the NUM estimated that a six day production cycle would increase output by 20%. But the result would be, they argued, the closure of 31 collieries and up to 26,000 job losses. They quoted a study of occupational stress ratings by the University of Manchester's Institute of Science and Technology which put miners at the top of the league and argued instead for a four-day working week and increased employment.[3]

The South Wales NUM made its opposition extremely clear when British Coal proposed to open a new pit at Margam on the basis of six-day working. Since Margam has never opened, however, the issue did not come to a head. At Asfordby, the mineworkers are represented by the Union of Democratic Mineworkers (UDM), which has taken a different view.

The argument over a six-day week in mining is, therefore, highly political and its resolution will depend on whatever future is won for an increasingly vulnerable industry.

Reclaiming flexibility

In 1987, Britain's largest union, the TGWU, launched its Link Up Campaign. Designed to attract part-time and temporary employees into union membership, the Campaign stressed the need for negotiators to seek full-time rights for part-time workers. By 1990, the union had succeeded in recruiting over 10,000 more women members at a time when male membership was falling.

A TGWU conference on equal opportunities and childcare in April 1989 and a subsequent negotiators' guide ('Putting Children in the Picture') both stressed the need for trades unions to 'reclaim flexibility'. The union explicitly accepted shorter and family-friendly working hours as well as increased childcare provision as strategies which would enable both men and women to combine employment with families. Implicit in this approach is a rejection of full-time employment as the ideal which requires universal full-time childcare provision to make it work.

For instance, the negotiators' guide notes: 'One solution is to extend the hours of childcare facilities. A second, and complementary, approach is to change the pattern of working hours to take account of family responsibilities. This means providing flexibility on workers' terms – not just to suit the convenience of employers.'[4] Thus, the union emphasises the need to negotiate improved maternity, paternity and family leave, and to enable mothers to return to work part-time, with an option to revert to full-time work later.

The different priorities of women with families are similarly reflected in a guide to 'Flexible Working' published recently by APEX, the office workers' union which is now part of the GMB general union. And in NUPE's Northern Ireland division, the recruitment of a large number of part-time public sector manual workers helped to transform the union's bargaining agenda.

> It became apparent that the union's traditional policy of prioritising wage claims in its negotiations was not benefiting part-time members. Because of the 'poverty trap' created by the National Insurance threshold, many actually found themselves worse off financially after a wage increase. . . . The part-time women members were much more concerned about other issues such as health and safety, leave provisions and minimum hours guarantees. A more effective way of increasing earnings for low-paid workers was to argue for their work to be revalued, a process which also had the effect of boosting the confidence of the workers concerned.[5]

One in ten members of the local government union, NALGO, works part-time and the union has also sought to change attitudes towards part-time employment. Its negotiating guidelines stress:

> Changing patterns of employment and the shift from manufacturing to service industries mean that part-time work is now a significant feature of the economy. Nonetheless part-time workers are still regarded as marginal to the 'real' (i.e., full-time) workforce and are grossly undervalued and underpaid. NALGO campaigns for part-timers to be treated as 'normal' members of staff and challenges employers' assumptions that part-time workers should put up with second-rate terms and conditions because they enjoy the 'luxury' of a job which fits in with their domestic responsibilities.[6]

In keeping with this general acceptance of part-time work, NALGO has encouraged its branches to seek job-sharing agreements with employers. The union advises negotiators to 'stand firm' on eight key points: the same terms and conditions for job-sharers as for full-time workers, on a *pro rata* basis; full union involvement when employers establish job-sharing arrangements; no down-grading of the conditions and pay attached to a full-time post; no reduction in the total number of full-time equivalent posts; job sharing to be initiated by employees, not imposed by employers; a written contract and job description for each job-sharer; a minimum 16-hour working week for job sharers, to safeguard the individual's rights to employment protection; and the right to return to full-time employment after a period of job sharing. Negotiators are also encouraged to try and open all posts at all levels to job sharing, with advertisements encouraging applications from job sharers, and training for personnel officers on the practicalities of job sharing.

Similar stipulations are offered to negotiators by the Banking, Insurance and Finance Union (BIFU). But there are striking differences in BIFU's basic approach towards part-time and non-standard working time arrangements – differences which reflect a more general debate within the trade union movement.

Conflicts between workers

For BIFU, part-time or flexible working is clearly a second-best to proper child care arrangements, rather than a complementary way of enabling members to balance employment and family. There are real fears that the child care campaign to which the union has given a high priority – in a sector where several leading employers have proved willing to invest in workplace nurseries – would be undermined by an equal emphasis on flexible working time.

Like NALGO, nearly one in ten BIFU members works part-time (from below 16 up to 29 hours a week). But part-time work is a recent development in banking, where full-time employment is still seen by the union as the norm. The rapid growth in part-time employment in the financial services sector over the last decade has created fears that 'real', full-time jobs would be lost – fears exacerbated by the rapid loss of jobs in the present recession.

In common with other unions, BIFU presses for *pro rata* terms and conditions for part-time employees. But innovative forms of part-time work – notably term-time and 'V-time' working – have proved more difficult to come to terms with. A research paper published by the union concludes that 'as long as all these caveats are borne in mind, term-time working can be a type of flexible working pattern that has benefits to BIFU members'.[7] The union's Executive Committee, however, has rejected both term-time and V-time working as flexible working options and instructed negotiators 'not to seek' either type of working. Where employers seek to 'impose' such arrangements, negotiators are urged to use the BIFU guidelines to protect their members.

BIFU's policy towards term-time and V-time working reflect the concerns of their full-time members. In the past, part-time workers were sometimes resented by full-time employees. The introduction of term-time staff gives rise to new fears: for instance, if temporary employees are needed to compensate for the absence of term-time staff during school holidays, then full-time employees could have to supervise the 'temps' and might no longer be allowed to take their holidays during the school holidays. Since not everyone can work during term-times, perhaps no-one should be allowed to.

V-time working – the option for full-time employees to reduce their hours and their pay (see p.32 above) – is seen as a threat to the general campaign for a shorter working week. Furthermore, if V-time allowed employees to take their reduced hours in the form of a longer (unpaid) holiday, then the effect could be to undermine negotiations for longer paid holidays for all staff. And remaining full-time employees might be required to compensate for the work not done by those who have reduced their hours.

In both cases, the perspective is clearly that of the full-time employees who constitute the large majority of BIFU members. As the composition of the union's membership changes, however, policy is likely to change as well. The increase in part-time employment and union membership was followed by a new emphasis on part-time workers' rights. Similarly, as new term-time employees join the union, and as existing full-time employees express a desire for term-time or V-time working, the union may find itself initiating such arrangements rather than merely responding to employers.

The 'no, unless' attitude adopted by the union's executive committee does, however, represent a real change from the position taken towards the introduction of Saturday working. When banks and building societies began to open on Saturday mornings in the late 1980s, the union refused to negotiate on the issue at all. It advised its members not to accept Saturday working, but left the matter to employers and individual employees. The result was a widespread move to Saturday working, with no union involvement in safeguarding individuals' pay or working conditions – illustrating a general danger for any union which tries to oppose working time changes which at least some of its members are prepared to accept.

Despite its emphasis on child care provision, BIFU has also responded to the introduction of 'career breaks' by the banks and other financial institutions (see p. 43 above). The union has sought to extend career breaks to all staff, not only those in senior management positions; to ensure that time spent on a career break counts towards pensionable service; and that those on career break are guaranteed employment at the end. In a recent sex discrimination case, BIFU successfully defended one of its members, Peggy Young, who was made redundant by Barclays Bank after working part-time for six months as a career break option. Mrs Young's severance pay was calculated on the basis of her part-time earnings, despite nearly 18 years' full-time service.

Formal acceptance or a new agenda?

From this review of several unions' policies, we can see clearly a general change in attitude towards part-time employment, from outright hostility to a new emphasis on recruitment and representation. Several factors explain the change, including the need to find new sources of membership and the influence of feminists within trade unions.

In 1988, a seminar in the Netherlands brought together women officials from several British and Dutch trades unions with academics and community activists. The report concluded:

> Faced with the strength of feeling from part-time and temporary women workers themselves, and the impossibility of achieving an outright ban in the present deregulatory climate, most of these arguments [i.e. against part-time and temporary working] have been formally lost, even though powerful informal rearguard action still remains in many cases. Most unions with a substantial female membership are now committed, at least on paper, to supporting such claims.[8]

Most unions, however, also continue to operate on the assumption of a 'normal' full-time working week and a 'normal' life-time of employment, with working time questions seen from the perspective of full-time employees. Tensions may arise between male trade union officials, many of whom continue to believe that they must be available 24 hours a day, and women officials for whom the work/family conflict is a daily reality. Some trade union equal rights committees and women's officers have challenged the prevailing assumptions and developed bargaining agendas which seek to integrate various forms of part-time employment and to make flexibility work for employees. And others have found, as the example from NUPE illustrated, that traditional pay bargaining is less important to women part-time employees than to full-time members.

Few trades unionists have embraced the more radical agenda of ending the distinction between 'full-time' and 'part-time' employment and promoting a wide range of working time arrangements on an equal footing. Similarly, few unions have reconsidered their view of lifetime career patterns.

The Civil Service unions, for instance, in their negotiations on new working patterns within the civil service sought and obtained an assurance from the Treasury that 'for the foreseeable future the traditional full-time career should remain the norm for the majority of civil servants'.[9] But should it? If unions, as well as managers, are to take the work/family question seriously, then they need to rethink career paths based on *continuous* full-time employment and create instead a new model which can embrace career breaks and periods of shorter hours working.

The logic of seeking equal rights for part-time employees, the spread of non-standard working hours and the pressure of the work/family debate all suggest, however, that unions will move towards a more fundamental review of their working time policies. Such a review will inevitably confront the conflict between collectively negotiated or individualised working hours.

Collective or individual working hours?

The engineering workers' campaign for shorter hours did not need to tackle the issue of a standard working time regime for all employees. Instead, the unions were able to use their collective strength to achieve a uniform change in collectively determined working conditions.

As we have seen, however, the collective determination of uniform working time is giving way in many other sectors to more varied, more individualised working time regimes. Furthermore, employment has been falling in manufacturing industries with high trade union membership and growing in the services where union organisation is often least effective. It is therefore not surprising that the trade union movement is often uncomfortable with working time arrangements which appear to challenge the whole collectivist basis of their existence.

In considering the strategic choice faced by trades unions, it is essential to distinguish between *uniform* working hours – everyone in the same job or occupation works the same hours – and *collectively* determined working time arrangements, where individuals' hours may vary within a generally agreed framework. Collective agreements within the engineering industry are an example of the first: the IRSF agreement within the Inland Revenue for voluntarily reduced working hours is an example of the second.

Essentially, the unions can respond to working time flexibility by using collective strength in an attempt to defend or to recreate uniform working hours; or they can use that collective strength to achieve a far wider choice of working hours for their individual members.

In Norway, where the trade union movement's hostility to part-time employment has meant very low levels of union membership amongst part-time employees, a union study of working time reform concluded:

> The further development and differentiation of time schedules represent a dilemma for the trade union movement. If it tries to continue with the system of the same time schedules for all (which has been the norm up to the present) the consequences will probably be that a number of individuals, groups or businesses break away and make adjustments outside the control of trades unions. If, on the other hand, the movement tries to achieve negotiated settlements with varying time schedules, it will probably run into problems trying to convince their core members in various areas.[10]

But the same study also stressed that:

> The normal working day, as an ideal and an institution which can be changed for a set price at set times, is possibly the most important resource that the trade union movement has in negotiations about working hours. But it does not suit all types of production and all stages of workers' lives, as a definitive schedule of working hours. One of the future balancing acts for the trade union movement will be to decide what proportion of workers may be allowed to deviate from the normal working day without undermining it.

The German study of working hours reform quoted earlier reached similar conclusions.[11]

Flexibility and union organisation

Achieving the right balance between defending standard working hours and accepting or even promoting working time flexibility is complicated by the implications of flexibility for union organisation itself. The widest variation in working time regimes is to be found in service occupations. Within the public sector, trade union organisation remains effective. But in retailing and other private services, trade union membership is often low. The operation of dozens of different working time contracts within one organisation not only makes a nonsense of traditional ideas of collectively-determined working hours, it also makes trade union organisation a nightmare. Organising trade union meetings during working hours, in a lunch-break or immediately after the end of a shift becomes impossible if employees are never all simultaneously at work.

Nonetheless, defending uniform working time arrangements is unlikely to be a successful strategy for the trades unions. Quite apart from economic considerations, employees clearly prefer greater choice and greater control over working hours, as well as shorter hours. Very few employees will give higher priority to union organisation than their own convenience. Other forms of union contact with members, including contact at home, will clearly be needed.

Some unions have already recognised the need, for instance, to move union meetings from male-dominated pubs to community centres. More fundamentally, trades unionists have begun to recognise that the workplace itself cannot be the central focus of organisation for part-time, temporary and casual employees. Thus, unions and community groups have collaborated in new initiatives, such as homeworkers' centres or 'pre-union' campaigns aimed at mothers before they are recruited to work in new shopping centres and other developments.[12]

Trade union policy also needs to distinguish between labour market deregulation and greater working time flexibility. As I argued in chapter 6, a new legislative framework of regulation is needed to maximise the advantages – and minimise the disadvantages – of working time flexibility. Similarly, at the industry and workplace level, trades unions need to seek a negotiated framework to maximise the benefits which working time flexibility can offer their members. Furthermore, until the British government or the European Community legislates for stronger health and safety protection, equal rights for part-time workers and protection for those with families, these can only be achieved through trade union negotiation.

Many unions have already succeeded in harmonising terms and conditions for part-time workers on a *pro rata* basis with full-time employees. And unions will inevitably have to play a defensive role against unacceptable forms of working time flexibility, such as 'on call' arrangements or 'zero hours' contracts which leave individuals with no clear employment status and wholly unpredictable working hours.

New working time agendas

It is equally important, however, that trades unions should initiate their own working time agendas. Depending on the nature of the occupation and the membership involved, unions could build on their present policies to create 'packages' of working time reform which would not only offer greater choice to individuals but would also provide a basis for solidarity between different groups of members. Packages of this kind would recognise the links between working time priorities and life-cycle stages (see p. 81).

For instance, a union might seek to win support for a right for all employees to move to shorter hours working within their present occupation, with priority given to parents of young children, those responsible for other dependants and those approaching retirement age. (Terms and conditions would be *pro rata* with full time workers and the right to return to full-time work after an agreed period would be preserved.)

Such an approach need not conflict with the aim of cutting working hours for everybody. If the standard working week is 40 hours, someone electing to work 30 hours would receive 75% of full pay; a reduction in the standard working week to 38 hours would mean that the person working 30 hours would receive 79% of full pay (or alternatively, that the employee on 75% of full pay could reduce working hours to 38½). For instance, the agreement for a shorter working week at Lucas Engine Management Systems specified that part-time employees, instead of having their hours reduced further, would receive a proportionate increase in their hourly pay from 20/39ths to 20/37ths of the full-time rate.

In some workplaces, the campaign for shorter working hours could lend itself to a 'menu' of options to suit different individual preferences. For instance, a general cut of two hours in the working week could be offered in the form of an early finish on Fridays, two weeks' extra holidays or the right to accumulate a longer leave period (a 'sabbatical') after several years.

Unions could also consider new ways of offering their members greater trade-offs between time and money within the pay bargaining round. Time-money trade-offs are not generally attractive at a time of high interest and mortgage rates. But they offer real advantages to people whose time budgets are more stressed than their financial budgets – whether an older worker whose mortgage is small or paid off, and whose children are grown up; or a parent whose need for time with children is even greater than the need for more money; or a younger person who wants a longer holiday now. Even if only a few people decide to trade part or all of their wage rise for shorter working hours, that is no reason not to offer the choice.

Similarly, unions could also take the initiative in pressing for the development of pension schemes into 'time banks' of the kind described in the previous chapter. Where an occupational pension scheme was extended in this way, a union could consider negotiating for additional contributions to be paid by employers.

A survey of members' working time preferences would help unions build on the information provided in this report and elsewhere. Thus armed, trade unions could expand existing policies on work/family relationships or initiate the Working Time Audit proposed in the previous chapter.

Furthermore, a union which found a wide diversity of working time preferences amongst its members could even consider the option of negotiating an agreement which offered all its members individual working hours contracts. Obviously, the work of the organisation, department or unit would have to be amenable to such an approach. But the individualised working time contracts in Norwegian hospitals and German department stores (see p.46 above) are not fundamentally different from the shift systems which industrial trades unions have always negotiated.

Instead of resisting this form of individualisation, a union could take the initiative in establishing a framework of agreed procedures, terms and conditions, and legal rights within which individuals could have far greater choice of working hours. The first step in such negotiations would be to organise the work of the enterprise into a variety of 'shifts' or working time arrangements. When it came to offering people a choice of arrangements, a union could reflect the interests of employees with particular needs. For instance, those caring for dependent children or elderly relatives on their own could be offered first choice of working hours, followed by those sharing family responsibilities with a partner, followed by those nearing retirement age. The working time arrangements which proved least popular to these groups would then attract an 'anti-social hours' premium, compensating employees who were left with little or no choice about their hours.

The apparent contradiction between trade unions' collective strength and the growing variety and individualisation of working time patterns need not be a contradiction at all. Instead, the challenge to the trade union movement is to find new ways of using their collective strength to achieve benefits which different people will enjoy in different ways at different times of their lives.

CONCLUSION

Our grandparents and parents could take for granted the way in which work would shape their days, their weeks, their years and even their lifetimes. The routines varied for men and women and from occupation to occupation. But the point is that they were *routines*, largely invisible and unquestioned, except when a conflict with the employer brought them to the surface – or unemployment, by banishing them, made them cruelly visible.

Today, few routines can be taken for granted. I wrote this book in order to establish how the organisation of working time and the shape of people's working lives are changing. The changes I have described are transforming full-time, life-time – male – employment into new patterns of flexible employment. They have made the 'normal' working day in a 'normal' working week a minority pursuit. And they have made obsolete the assumptions on which employment law and social security systems are founded. These changes in working time are, inevitably, uneven and incomplete. But they are real. They are part of much bigger changes in the lives of women and, therefore, of men; in the structure of economies; the technology of production and communications; and the organisation of industries and services. The transformation of working time itself is one of the elements which defines a modern, 'post-industrial' society.

The issue, then, is not whether working time is changing, but what we do about these changes. For some, any reduction in full-time, life-time employment is a threat to the security of individuals and families; part-time and flexible employment are new forms of exploitation to be accepted grudgingly, if at all. Full-time, core jobs must be preferred to, and protected against, flexible, 'peripheral' employment. But this defence of the old ignores the real opportunities and benefits offered by the new: benefits to enterprises and the economy in the form of higher productivity, benefits to individuals and families in the form of greater choice and a better fit between work and home.

Instead of resisting flexibility, we will do better to make it work for us. Indeed, by making working time issues visible, we can find a new way to approach some of the large questions which are central to the modern political agenda, not least the agenda for European social democracy.

Take, for instance, the issue of full employment. Previously, full employment meant – explicitly or implicitly – full-time, life-time employment. *Real* employment. Men's employment. In the 1950s, it was British and other European men who enjoyed full employment, while married women with children left the labour market. In the mid-1980s, when unemployment was falling, Opposition spokesmen routinely denounced each month's figures on the grounds that most of the new jobs were 'only part-time'. Today, there can be no adequate definition of full employment unless it incorporates the demand for part-time work at various stages of millions of people's lives.

The economic strategies needed to achieve modern full employment are outside the scope of this book. It is important to stress, however, that if shorter working hours are linked to and financed by productivity gains (as in most of the examples I have found), then they are not a route to lower unemployment. Indeed, Fritz Scharpf, one of Germany's leading political scientists, has argued that full employment can only be recovered 'through a redistribution of existing work opportunities and working incomes at the expense of the great majority of those who are presently employed.'[1] There is plenty of work which needs to be done, much of it caring for other people; doing it can help to contribute to economic growth; but, one way or another, it has to be paid for.

But how we organise working time and how we define full employment reaches deep into the question of the kind of economy, the kind of society we want to live in. Throughout this book, I have stressed three kinds of questions. The first concerns production and how Britain and other Western economies create competitive enterprises. The second concerns gender, the relationships between women and men, between work and family. The third concerns welfare, particularly the provision of care for children and elderly dependants. However disparate they may appear, they are in fact intimately linked.

First, the change in working time is central to the creation of a modern economy. Our ability to enjoy high and rising standards of living, to improve our quality of life, increase our leisure time and finance good public services all depend upon the economy's productive capacity. As Harvard Business School analyst, Michael Porter, argues:

> The only meaningful concept of competitiveness at the national
> level is national productivity. A rising standard of living depends on
> the capacity of a nation's firms to achieve high levels of pro-

ductivity and to increase productivity over time. . . . cheap labour
and a 'favourable' exchange rate are not meaningful definitions of
competitiveness. The aim is to support high wages and command
premium prices in international markets.'[2]

Porter is no social democrat, but his is a vision of high-skill, high-tech,
high-wage economies which European and Scandinavian social democrats
share.

As we have seen throughout this book, the drive to improve productivity is central to the reorganisation of working time. In order to
increase the return on expensive capital equipment while meeting
employees' demands for shorter hours, individuals' working hours are
decoupled from those of factories. Plants work longer than people. In
order to meet customers' needs for services at most and sometimes all
hours of the day and night, employees on part-time, annual hours or
individualised hours contracts replace those working rigid, full-time
hours. Services work longer than people.

But there is more to the change in working hours than that. Modern
economies depend upon human knowledge. Quality of people is even
more important than quality of plant. But as fulfilling a routine becomes
less valuable to the enterprise than the individual's knowledge, experience
and ability to take responsibility, then the individual becomes more likely
– and more able – to resist a working time routine. As goods and services
become more individualised, so do the skills needed to produce them, and
so too does the time in which they are produced.

Of course, that does not mean that we all suddenly control our work.
Length of working hours and working time autonomy are complex
indicators of employment status. In Britain, a manager may combine
extremely long hours with high status, high financial rewards and
considerable autonomy over the organisation and execution of his work.
For a skilled industrial worker, shorter hours may operate within a rigid
pattern of shifts and holidays, while a shop assistant may trade short,
part-time hours for lower pay and occupational welfare. Nonetheless, at
least in industry, cuts in working hours are often integrally linked to the
need for more flexibly skilled, more productive team workers.

The part-time employee who will only take a job if the hours are right
and the self-employed professional who organises her own hours of work
have in common some real control over their time. Both place a high
value on the organisation of their time. As more people come to expect
that they will make conscious decisions about the shape of their lives,
then they will become more demanding workers as well as more

demanding consumers. And as employers compete to attract and retain educated, skilled and experienced workers, then a choice of working hours will be added to pay, perks and attractive workplaces as inducements to employees.

All this suggests some fundamental changes in the relationship between work and the rest of our lives. It is the hours spent at work which make non-work – leisure, family, retirement – possible. Production finances social reproduction and consumption. (In the old gender division of labour, of course, it was the man's working time which financed the time spent by the woman at home: and the woman's time at home which made the man's working time possible.) Shorter working hours produce more time for family, leisure and other activities. It is a commonplace of modern economies that as people spend less time producing and more time consuming, they become more demanding consumers. But what we are now beginning to see in the part-time employee as well as the self-employed professional is a consumer attitude towards production time itself. Just as we decide (with more or less freedom, depending on our income and other constraints) how we will spend our leisure, so we can begin to decide how much of our time, and when, will be 'consumed' by work.

Women's lives, men's lives

Second, working time changes are being driven, in part, by the change which women are demanding and creating in their own lives. It is not surprising that, as women win access to better education, higher pay and greater responsibility (and as marriage becomes a riskier bet), they spend more time in employment and less at home. But this is more than a question of women demanding the right to use their abilities and earn their living.

An economy which is increasingly dependent upon the quality of its human capital needs to find ways of employing its women. The failure of a modern economy to employ large numbers of women with children – particularly women who have already acquired a high level of education[3] – suggests profound structural inefficiencies as well as social inadequacies. There are many reasons why women's employment cannot always be substituted for men's. But an economy which appears to be successful in other ways may be operating below its productive capacity if it is employing (some) men with less education or potential than (some) women who are caring for children.

But women do not participate in the labour market on the same terms as men. For most men, combining work and family is an assumption on which they can plan their lives. For most women, it is a problem which affects their lives not only while children are young but before they are born and after they grow up.

As I have argued throughout this book, the male organisation of working time is incompatible with the care of children and other dependants. Opportunity at work is inseparable from responsibility at home. As long as responsibility is unequally shared at home, strategies for equality at work will remain fatally flawed. Slowly, however, the gap between women's and men's domestic work is beginning to shrink. As men spend less time in paid work and women spend more, the reverse is happening to housework, with women doing less and men doing more. And with women's housework time falling, along with men's paid work time, the time both spend in childcare has begun to increase.

The conflict between work and family is not a question which employers can afford to ignore any longer. To their credit, many have begun to acknowledge the problem. In Britain today, half our new graduates are women, as are half of newly-qualified doctors and lawyers, one-third of accountants and a growing proportion of other professionals. Within the next two decades, they will have to find answers to the conflict between work and family: and the men and women who employ and manage them cannot afford to lose their services.

Third, there is the question of how we organise the care of young and old.[4] In traditionally-organised industrial economies, women fill the gap between male work and family welfare. As women move into employment, the gap becomes visible; and the more women follow the pattern of men's working lives, the bigger the gap becomes.

It may be, quite literally, a gap in the lives of children who return to empty homes between the end of school and the arrival of a parent. (About a quarter of a million British children are left unattended after school each day.[5]) The gap may be filled by services – whether government, private, employer or voluntary – which care for children and sick or otherwise dependent adults. Or the gap may be avoided by the woman refusing to work male hours, or the man reorganising his own, so that the work time of at least one adult in the household fits their family responsibilities.

For at least the last two decades, campaigners and policy-makers have stressed the unmet need for childcare services. But even in Sweden, with a very high level of public childcare provision, there remain unmet needs for childcare. Furthermore, provision for paid time off (maternity, paternity, parental and family leave, as well as sick leave) is so extensive that one Swedish economist, Gosta Esping-Andersen, reports that on any one day about half of Swedish women in employment are not in fact at work.

In Sweden, the high level of welfare services which makes possible a very high level of employment amongst women depends upon a level of taxation to which, as the recent election results suggest, there is growing resistance. In Britain, with grossly inadequate childcare and other welfare services, there may be less resistance to taxation than commonly believed (at the last election, over half of voters supported parties which proposed some increase in income tax). Furthermore, an expansion in childcare services would, after a decade or so, more than pay for itself through the taxes and contributions of women returning to employment.[6] Nonetheless, the high-tax/high-service/high-female-employment route clearly faces political difficulties.

An alternative route to high levels of female employment, which we can see in the USA, is the purchase of childcare services through the private market, possibly assisted by some form of tax relief. It is an option which depends, first, upon a large pool of low-paid women for whom no other employment is available, often because they have children of their own and no-one else to care for them, and, second, upon an absence of regulation about working hours and wages. In America, Black and Hispanic women – including Mexican women who are vulnerable to migration checks – provide a large part of the country's new domestic servants. Not only does private childcare depend upon this racially segregated workforce, but it produces highly stratified childcare services, with a growing gap between services for the children of lower-income and higher-income families.

In Britain, a model which depends upon full-time services to enable women to work full-time male hours simply does not fit most women's aspirations. Instead of forgoing some of their earnings to secure private or public services to care for their children, the majority of women forgo some of their earnings to secure the time which enables them to care for their children themselves.

The trade-off between earnings and children remains, to a large extent, an individual decision, and the individuals making it remain almost entirely women. For lone parents, it will remain an individual decision, although one which should be facilitated by social security reform. For others, it is also a household and family question, as more and more families depend upon a combination of full-time and part-time earnings. Social and personal expectations make it more difficult for a man to consider such a trade-off; and, despite the growth in the number of women earning more than their partners, the continuation of unequal pay creates a real disincentive for both women and men to work less than full-time hours.

Here is a central task for public policy as well as for employers: to create opportunities for men *and* women to organise their working hours so that they can have more time for their families as well as for themselves. Of course, more services are needed for children outside the hours and years of school, as well as for many older people, and those services must take account of the growing variety of working time patterns. But strategies which enable adults to make their own trade-offs between time and money may well prove more politically acceptable than those which depend upon a high level of general taxation to finance, through welfare services, one particular way of using adults' time.

The revolution which is taking place in the organisation of work requires a revolution in the thinking of legislators, employers and trade unions.

If working hours are regulated on the basis of standard, rigid patterns, then people's ability to shape their own lives is reduced and enterprises' abilities to compete undermined. But if working hours are deregulated in the name of the 'free market', then millions of people lose their ability to withstand the excessive demands of their employers, and their own health and safety (as well as the safety of some of the people they serve) are jeopardised.

That is why I have argued for a new form of regulation, based on a new principle of 'fair flexibility', which will encourage a growing variety of working time arrangements, while creating justified limits on what some employers and, indeed, some employees would otherwise wish to do. In line with the European Community's new Working Time Directive, I propose a new British Working Time Act which would guarantee every employee four weeks' paid holidays a year, with a thirteen-hour limit on the average working day and a 5½ day limit on the average working week. In place of the increasingly artificial distinctions between full-time and part-time workers, I propose that Britain extends the same rights, on a *pro rata* basis, to all employees regardless of the hours they work, and makes unemployment benefit available, also *pro rata*, to part-time workers. And instead of the absurd confusion of Britain's present Sunday trading laws, I propose substantial deregulation of Sunday shopping coupled with effective protection for retail workers.

New thinking needs to extend to the shape of the working lifetime as well as the working day and week. Compulsory retirement and extensive discrimination on the grounds of age make it impossible for individuals to create working lifetimes to suit their own needs and circumstances. We need, therefore, to extend employment protection laws at least to the age

171

of 70, as a prelude to an age discrimination law, and to introduce part-time pensions as part of a flexible decade of retirement.

This sweeping reform of employment and social security law is essential to ensure that millions of flexible workers are not treated as second-class citizens. But it will also help achieve a larger goal: to create an economy where more and more people can choose the working hours they want, where a growing number of jobs are available with a growing variety of working time arrangements, where the offer of a job increasingly comes with the choice of hours.

Employers who have been used to determining and managing standardised working hours – and unions who have been used to negotiating them – may recoil from a new vision of widely variable working hours. But new working time arrangements are the product of employers' continuing search for higher productivity and higher profits, in a world where men want to reduce their employment hours and women to increase theirs. As employers confront their inability to secure equal opportunities for women – and thus to maximise their use of human capital – I believe they will have to accept the new challenge of radically re-organising working hours, using information technology to offer women and men a wide variety of working time contracts. For unions too, recruiting and representing an increasingly disparate workforce will depend upon their ability to use collective organisation to achieve more – rather than less – individualisation of working conditions.

Different working hours for different people at different stages of their lives. That is not a nightmare of exploitation, but a way of giving all of us more control over our lives.

This new approach needs politicians who understand that how we look after families is just as much a political issue as how we create a competitive economy – and that the two things go together. It needs the European Community and national governments to create a new frame-work of social security and employment law. It needs employers who can seize the opportunities offered to raise productivity through working time reorganisation. It needs unions who understand that bargaining about time can be as important as bargaining about money.

And it needs all of them – and all of us – to think again about the way in which work is divided between men and women, and the way in which we divide our lives between work and everything else.

NOTES

Introduction

1 Catherine Marsh, *Hours of Work of Women and Men in Britain*, Equal Opportunities Commission, HMSO, 1991.
2 *Social Trends 20*, HMSO, 1990, Table 4.12.
3 B.A. Hepple in R. Blanpain and E. Kohler (eds), *Legal and Contractual Limitations to Working-Time in the European Community Member States*, European Foundation, the Netherlands, Kluwer, 1988.
4 D. Miliband, *Learning by Right*, IPPR, 1990.
5 *Social Trends*, op.cit., Table 2.6. In 1987, 44% of people lived in households consisting of a married couple with dependent children; the next largest group, 29%, lived as married couples without dependent children.
6 E.P. Thompson, 'Time, Work Discipline and Industrial Capitalism' in *Past and Present*, 38, December 1967, p.93.
7 David R. Roediger and Philip S. Foner, *Our Own Time: A History of American Labor and the Working Day*, London/New York, Verso, 1989, p.1.
8 F. Block, *Postindustrial Possibilities*, Berkeley, CA, University of California Press, 1990, discusses the idea of a 'post-industrial' life cycle.
9 Lynda Bransbury, *Escaping from Dependency: Welfare strategies for working parents*, London, Rivers Oram Press/IPPR, forthcoming.

1 Working Lifetimes and Working Hours

1 Charles Handy, *The Age of Unreason*, London, Century Hutchinson, 1989, pp.37–8.
2 Peter Elias and Brian Main, *Women's Working Lives: Evidence from the National Training Survey*, Institute for Employment Research, 1982.
3 J. Martin and C. Roberts, *Women and Employment: A Lifetime Perspective* (Report of the 1980 DE/OPCS Women and Employment Survey), HMSO 1984.
4 T. Schuller and A. Walker, *The Time of Our Life*, IPPR, 1990, Table 4.
5 'Staying on at work becomes an old fashion in the west', *Financial Times*, 22 July 1992.
6 Elias and Main, *Women's Working Lives*, op.cit.

7 S. Dex, *Women's Work Histories: an analysis of the Women and Employment Survey*, Research Paper 46, Department of Employment 1984. Her employment histories are discussed and elaborated upon by J. Brannen and P. Moss, *Managing Mothers: Dual Earner Households After Maternity Leave*, London, Unwin Hyman, 1991.

8 Martin and Roberts, *Women and Employment*, op.cit., Tables 9.1 and 9.14. Employment rates for 30–34 year-olds increased from 37% to 56% and for 35–39 year-olds from 46% to 69%, comparing those born in 1920–24 with those born in 1960–64.

9 S. McRae and W.W. Daniel, *Maternity Rights: The Experience of Women and Employers*, Policy Studies Institute, London, 1991.

10 The PSI survey only included women who were in employment when they became pregnant. The Women and Employment Survey included those not working before pregnancy who were, unsurprisingly, less likely to start working after the child's birth. Nonetheless, both surveys produced comparable figures for the late 1970s (the Women and Employment Survey found 17% of those having first babies in 1975–79 had returned to work within 6 months; PSI found 20% of mothers having babies in 1979 had returned to work within 9 months.) The comparison between the two surveys may nonetheless slightly overstate the changes involved.

11 Martin and Roberts, *Women's Employment*, op.cit., Table 9.5.

12 *Social Trends 20*, HMSO 1990, Table 4.3.

13 Henley Centre for Forecasting, *Family Futures*, 1989.

14 *Employment Gazette*, Vol.100 no.6, June 1992, London: HMSO, Table 1.1.

15 Martin and Roberts, *Women and Employment*, op.cit., Table 9.1.

16 Office of Population Censuses and Surveys, *Labour Force Survey 1988 and 1989*, London, HMSO, 1991, Table 5.9.

17 Martin and Roberts, *Women's Employment*, op.cit., Tables 9.1 and 9.11.

18 McRae and Daniel, *Maternity Rights*, op.cit., Fig.3.

19 Department of Employment Gazette, March 1988 and June 1992.

20 Department of Employment, *New Earnings Survey 1991*, London, HMSO, Tables 148 and 149.

21 Marsh, *Hours of Work*, op.cit., Table 3.1.

22 Eurostat, 1990.

23 Analysis by USDAW of the New Earnings Survey 1988.

24 All information in this section from Martin Campbell and Michael Daly, 'Self-employment: into the 1990s', *Employment Gazette*, June 1992.

25 *Employment Gazette*, March 1987.

26 Low Pay Unit, *The New Review*, 1991, no.8.

27 Paul Rathkey, *Time and Work: Employee Preferences and Policy Options*, Jim Conway Memorial Foundation, September 1988, p.84.

28 ACAS, *Labour Flexibility in Britain*, 1987.

29 S. Horrell, J. Rubery and B. Burchell, *Working-Time Patterns, Constraints*

and Preferences, Department of Applied Economics, University of Cambridge, July 1989.

30 Marsh, *Hours of Work*, Table 7.1 and p.49.
31 *Social Trends 20*, Table 10.1.

2 New Ways of Working

1 ACAS, *Labour Flexibility*, op.cit.
2 Rathkey, *Time and Work*, op.cit.
3 *AEU Journal*, September 1989, p.35.
4 Conversation with the author, June 1992.
5 *AEU Journal*, July 1990.
6 Income Data Services, *Reorganising Working Time*, September 1988, pp.18, 21.
7 'Negotiating Shorter Working Hours in the European Community', *Bulletin of European Shiftwork Topics*, no.1, September 1989, European Foundation for the Improvement of Living and Working Conditions, p.12.
8 Labour Research Department, *Bargaining Report*, February 1988.
9 Labour Research Department, *Bargaining Report 65* (September 1987) and 76 (September 1988).
10 *Bulletin of European Shiftwork Topics*, Fig.5.3.
11 *Equal Opportunities for Women in the Civil Service: Programme of Action*, Cabinet Office (Management and Personnel Office), February 1984.
12 Cabinet Office, *Equal Opportunities for Women in the Civil Service: Progress Report 1990–1991*, London, HMSO, 1991.
13 *Home Office v Ms G.S.I. Holmes*, [1984] ICR 678, [1984] IRLR 299.
14 Friederike Maier, 'Part-time Work, Social Security Protections and Labour Law: an International Comparison', Berlin, WZB, 1989.
15 ILO, *Conditions of Work Digest*.
16 Centre for Research on European Women, *Infrastructures and women's employment*, European Commission, 1990, Tables 5.1 and 5.3.
17 See also Walker and Schuller, *The Time of Our Life*, op. cit.
18 ILO, *Conditions of Work Digest*.
19 ACAS, *Labour Flexibility*, op.cit.
20 'New Ways to Work', *Job Sharing and Companies*, and *Newsletter*, Spring 1989.
21 *Managing change: the organisation of work*, CBI, 1985, p.16.
22 *Financial Times*, 9 October 1985.
23 Chris Curson (ed.), *Flexible Patterns of Work*, Institute of Personnel Management, 1986, p.43.
24 *New Proposed Working Practices in the British Deep Coal Mining Industry*, Report presented to NUM Conference, 1987, National Union of Mineworkers 1987.
25 IDS, *Reorganising Working Time*, op.cit., p.22.

26 Rathkey, *Time and Work*, op.cit., p.98.
27 European Trade Union Institute, *Newsletter*, July 1992.
28 R. Blanpain and E. Kohler (eds), *Legal and Contractual Limitations to Working-Time in the European Community Member States*, European Foundation for the Improvement of Living and Working Conditions, The Netherlands, Kluwer 1988, p.84.
29 ILO, *Conditions of Work Digest*, p.206.
30 Marsh, *Hours of Work*, op.cit., p.18.
31 *Financial Times*, 7 November 1990.
32 IDS, *Reorganising Working Time*, op.cit., p.16.
33 'Negotiations between Imperial Chemical Industries plc and the Signatory Unions in Respect of Weekly Staff', ICI Group Personnel Department, 7 May 1991.
34 *Financial Times*, 6 February 1991.
35 IDS, *Reorganising Working Time*, op.cit., p.13.
36 Martin Wroe, 'Leaner, meaner, but ready for bids', *Independent*, 27 March 1991.
37 Marsh, *Hours of Work*, op.cit., p.55.
38 Horrell and Rubery, *Employers' Working-Time Policies*, op.cit., p.35.
39 Lloyds Bank Ltd v Secretary of State for Employment [1979] ICR 258. For a discussion of this and other relevant cases, see Bob Hepple, *Working Time: A New Legal Framework?*, IPPR, 1990.
40 ILO, *Conditions of Work Digest*, op.cit., p.217.
41 Incomes Data Services, *Maternity and Paternity Leave (Study 351)*, London, 1985.
42 Centre for Research on European Women, *Infrastructures and Women's Employment*, Table 5.1.
43 P. Moss and J. Brannen, 'Fathers' employment' in C. Lewis and M. O'Brien (eds) *Reassessing Fatherhood: New Observations on Fathers and the Modern Family*, London, Sage, 1987.
44 R. Rapoport and P. Moss, *Exploring Ways of Integrating Men and Women as Equals at Work*, 1989.
45 *Sunday Times* 18 February 1990.

3 The Second Shift: Work in the Home

1 A. Oakley, *Housewife*, Harmondsworth, Penguin, 1974.
2 See, for instance, Oakley, *Housewife* op.cit.; Arlie Hochschild with Anne Machung, *The Second Shift: Working Parents and the Revolution at Home*, London, Piatkus, 1990; and Julia Brannen and Peter Moss, *Managing Mothers*, London, Unwin Hyman, 1991.
3 M. Young and P. Willmott, *The Symmetrical Family*, London, Routledge and Kegan Paul, 1973.

4 Jonathan Gershuny, *The Economy of Time*, Oxford University Press (forthcoming).

5 Social and Community Planning Research, *British Social Attitudes, Cumulative Sourcebook*, Aldershot, Gower, 1992, Tables N.2–4.

6 Martin and Roberts, *Women and Employment*, op.cit., Table 8.7. For technical reasons, this survey may have overestimated the extent of men's involvement in domestic work.

7 Cathy Clift and Daryl Fielding, *The Balance of Power*, Lowe Howard-Spink 1991.

8 Roger Jowell et al. (eds), *British Social Attitudes: the 5th report*, Gower, Aldershot, 1988, Table 10.2.

9 SCPR, op.cit., Table 10.2.

10 J. Brannen and P. Moss, *Managing Mothers: Dual Earner Households after Maternity Leave*, London, Unwin Hyman, 1991, pp.159–77.

11 Martin and Roberts, *Women and Employment*, op.cit., pp.38–9.

12 S. Witherspoon, 'Working Mothers', in R. Jowell, et al. (eds), *British Social Attitudes: The 8th Report*, SCPR/Dartmouth 1991.

13 S. Witherspoon, 'Interim Report: A Woman's Work', in R. Jowell et al. (eds), *British Social Attitudes: The 5th Report*, SCPR/Gower 1988, Table 10.2.

14 Horrell, *Working Time Patterns*, op.cit.

15 Thore K. Karlsen, *Arbeidstid og fleksibilitet i arbeidslivet* ('Working Time and Flexibility in Employment'), Oslo, FAFO, May 1989.

16 Jonathan Gershuny, *Changing Times* (Report to the European Foundation for the Improvement of Living and Working Conditions), and private communications with the author.

17 J. Gershuny, 'Are We Running Out of Time?' in *Futures*, Jan/Feb 1992.

18 Gershuny, *Changing Times*, op.cit., p.205.

19 D. Piachaud, *Round About Fifty Hours a Week: The Time Costs of Children*, 1984, London, Child Poverty Action Group.

20 *Social Trends 20*, Table 1.2.

21 OPCS, *Informal Carers*, HMSO, 1985.

22 Martin and Roberts, *Women and Employment*, op.cit., p.113.

23 J. Gershuny, S. Jones and M. Godwin, *The Allocation of Time within the Household*, Report to the Unilever Household Reseach Project, Unilever, November 1989, figs 1.7 and 1.8.

4 How People Feel About Working Time

1 Bob Tyrrell, 'Anticipating the Culture of the 1990s', in *Annual Review of Social Change*, Henley Centre, March 1991.

2 Sharon Witherspoon and Gillian Prior, 'Working mothers: Free to choose?' in Roger Jowell, et al. (eds), *British Social Attitudes, 8th report*, SCPR/Dartmouth, 1991.

3 Marsh, *Hours of Work*, op.cit., Table 10.3.

4 Horrell, et al., *Working Time Patterns*, op.cit., Table 17.
5 Marsh, *Hours of Work*, op.cit., Table 9.1.
6 Martin and Roberts, *Women and Employment*, op.cit., p.63.
7 Marsh, *Hours of Work*, op.cit., Table 9.4.
8 'Working Mothers Survey', BhS with the Working Mothers Association, London, March 1992.
9 Martin and Roberts, *Women and Employment*, op.cit., p.41.
10 Horrell, *Working Time Patterns*, op.cit., p.12.
11 Witherspoon, 'Working Mothers', op.cit.
12 Martyn Halsall, 'A workforce raring to go if someone would let it', *Guardian*, 24 September 1990.
13 Witherspoon, 'Working Mothers', op.cit., p.134.
14 Marsh, *Hours of Work*, op.cit., Table 10.3.
15 Rathkey, *Time and Work*, op.cit., Table 33.
16 Marsh, *Hours of Work*, op.cit., Table 10.5.
17 McRae and Daniel, *Maternity Rights*, op.cit., Fig.10.
18 Rathkey, *Time and Work*, op.cit., pp.66–8.
19 *Working Hours' Reforms*, Norwegian Official Report 1987, 9E, Oslo, Fig.0.2.
20 Karlsen, *Arbeidstid*, op.cit., pp.13–14.
21 Marsh, *Hours of Work*, op.cit., p.75 and Table 10.3.
22 Rathkey, *Time and Work*, op.cit., p.74.
23 Horrell, *Working Time Patterns*, op.cit., Table 18.
24 Marsh, *Hours of Work*, op.cit., Table 10.4.
25 Press release, Keep Sunday Special Campaign, 28 February 1990.
26 Parliamentary brief, Shopping Hours Reform Council, January 1991.
27 Marsh, *Hours of Work*, op.cit., Tables 6.5 and 10.4.
28 Hartmut Seifert, '*Soizialvertragliche Arbeitszeitgestaltung: Ein neues Konzept der Arbeitszeitpolitik?*' (Socially acceptable organisation of working time: A new concept of working time politics?') Berlin in *WSI Mitteilungen*, 11/1989, p.21.
29 McRae and Daniel, *Maternity Rights*, op.cit., Fig.10.
30 Karlsen, *Arbeidstid*, op.cit.

5 Time to Change

1 Letter to the *Independent*, 1 March 1990.
2 B. Wedderburn, *Studies on shiftwork in the steel industry*, Edinburgh 1976, cited in *Flexibility of Working Time in Western Europe*, European Trade Union Institute, 1986.
3 G. Aronsson, K. Barklof, B. Gardell, 'The Working Environment of Local Traffic Personnel', University of Stockholm Institute of Psychology Report no.26, 1980.
4 G. Hildebrandt, W. Rogmert and J. Rutenfranz, 'The influence of fatigue and

rest period on the circadian variation of error frequency in shiftworers (engine drivers)' in W.P. Colquhoun (ed.), *Experimental studies in shift work*, Westdeutscher Verlag, 1975.

5 Wisner and J. Carpentier, *Le Travail Poste*, (Report to the Ministry of Labour), Paris, January 1979.

6 Japan Association of Industrial Health, 'Opinion on night work and shift work', *Journal of Science of Labour*, 1979, vol.55, no.8, Part II, pp.1–36.

7 See, for a review, H. Seifert, '*Sozialvertragliche Arbeitszeitgestaltung*', WSI Mitteilungen 11/1989, Berlin 1989.

8 A. Hidden, *Investigation into the Clapham Junction Railway Accident*, Department of Transport, HMSO 1989, Paragraphs 8.54, 16.11, 16.13.

9 'The HJSC Hours of Work Campaign – A Note by the Secretariat,' British Medical Association 1990; *British Medical Journal*, vol.302, 22 June 1991.

10 *The Times*, 7 March 1990.

11 Blanpain and Kohler, *Legal and Contractual Limitations*, op.cit., p.79.

12 European Trade Union Institute 1986, op cit., p.55.

13 CBI, *Managing Change*, p.26.

14 M. White, *Shorter working time through national industry agreements*, London, Department of Employment Research paper 39, 1982.

15 H. Seifert, '*Beschaftigungswirkungen und Perspektiven der Arbeitszeitpolitik*', Berlin in WSI Mitteilungen 3/1989.

16 C. Curson (ed.), *Flexible Patterns of Work*, Institute of Personnel Management, 1986, p.189.

17 ILO, *Conditions of Work Digest*, p.284.

18 CBI, *Managing Change*, p.26.

19 Seifert, '*Beschaftigungswirkungen*', op.cit.

20 'Overtime Threat to Reduced Work Hours', TUC press release, 4 July 1988; Campaign for Reduced Working Time, TUC Progress Report 19, June 1988.

21 Curson, *Flexible Patterns*, op.cit., p.192.

22 *Employment Gazette*, 1988, 96, 11, pp.607–15.

23 Seifert, '*Sozialvertragliche*' op.cit.

24 A. Hochschild with A. Machung, *The Second Shift: Working Parents and the Revolution at Home*, London, Piatkus, 1990; and S.A. Hewlett, *When the Bough Breaks: The Cost of Neglecting Our Children*, New York, Basic Books, 1991.

25 S. Kamerman and A. Kahn (eds), *Child Care, Parental Leave, and the Under 3s: Policy Innovation in Europe*, Connecticut, Auburn House, 1991.

26 Marsh, *Hours of Work*, op.cit., p.25.

27 Martin and Roberts, *Women and Employment*, op.cit., Table 10.16.

28 H. Joshi, 'The Cash Opportunity Costs of Childbearing: An Approach to Estimation using British Data', *Population Studies*, 44, 1990.

29 Martin and Roberts, *Women and Employment*, op.cit., Tables 5.8, 5.9, 5.14, 5.15, 5.19, 5.25.

30 Catherine Hakim, 'Workforce Restructuring, Social Insurance Coverage and

the Black Economy', *Journal of Social Policy*, 1989, Vol.18, no.4, pp.471–503.

31 E. Garnsey, *The Provision and Quality of Part-time Work: The case of Great Britain and France*, Brussels, European Commission, 1984.

32 House of Commons, *Part-time work*, Employment Committee second report, House of Commons paper 122-I, Session 1989–1990, London, HMSO, 1990.

33 European Trade Union Institute, *Collective Bargaining in Western Europe in 1990 and Prospects for 1991*, Brussels, 1991, p.78.

34 Basic Policy Programme of the Social Democratic Party of Germany, adopted 20 December 1989.

35 Horrell, *Working Time Patterns*, op.cit., pp.32–3.

36 Ruth Lister, *Women's economic dependency and social security*, Equal Opportunities Commission, Research Discussion Series no.2, 1992, pp.16–18.

37 *Family Expenditure Survey 1989*, HMSO, Table 21.

38 Anna Coote, Harriet Harman and Patricia Hewitt, *The Family Way*, IPPR, 1990.

39 The 'mommy track' was the phrase coined to describe a management strategy outlined by Felice N. Schwartz in a controversial article, 'Management Women and the New Facts of Life', *Harvard Business Review*, Jan–Feb 1989.

40 Peter Moss, speech to the Equal Opportunities Commission, Action Plan for Child Care, February 1991.

6 Fair Flexibility: Changing the Law

1 Based on Blanpain and Kohler (eds), *Working Time in the EC*, op.cit., pp.18–24.

2 Bob Hepple, *Working Time: A New Legal Framework?*, op.cit.

3 'Britain wins opt-out on EC work hours law', *Independent*, 25 June 1992.

4 Hepple, *Working Time*, op.cit.

5 Marsh, *Hours of Work*, op.cit., p.35; and personal communication with the EOC.

6 *Independent on Sunday*, 6 October 1991.

7 Marsh, *Hours of Work*, op.cit., Table 6.6.

8 The total week is 168 hours. From that we deduct the 35-hour break (one complete day off plus an 11-hour break on a second day), leaving 133 hours. Five further 11-hour breaks must be deducted, leaving 78 potential working hours.

9 Hepple, *Working Time*, op.cit., pp.13–15.

10 Martin and Roberts, *Women and Employment*, op.cit., Table 4.3.

11 Catherine Hakim, 'Employment Rights', op.cit.

12 Marsh, *Hours of Work*, op.cit., Tables 8.2 and 8.3, and author's calculations.

13 Horrell and Rubery, *Employers' Working-Time Policies*, op.cit., p.55.

14 Labour Party, *Meet the Challenge, Make the Change* (final report of Labour's Policy Review), p.22.

15 M. Syrett, *Employing Job Sharers, Part-Time and Temporary Staff*, Institute of Personnel Management, 1983, p.29.

16 *Family Friendly Working*, Institute of Manpower Studies, University of Sussex, July 1992.

17 Hepple, *Working Time*, op.cit., pp.17–19.

18 European Commission, Proposed draft directives on atypical working, (COM [90] 228-SYN 280-SYN281), Brussels, 26 June 1990.

19 Curson, *Flexible Patterns of Work*, op.cit., p.108.

20 Coote, Harman and Hewitt, *The Family Way*, op.cit.

21 Hewlett, *When the Bough Breaks*, op.cit.

22 Hepple, *Working Time*, op.cit., p.18.

23 Rapoport and Moss, *Integrating Men and Women*, op.cit., pp.22–5.

24 McRae and Daniel, *Maternity Rights*, op.cit., Fig.7.

25 Marsh, *Hours of Work*, op.cit., Table 7.1.

26 See T. Askham, T. Burke, D. Ramsden, *EC Sunday Trading Rules*, Butterworths 1990, for a detailed analysis of Sunday trading legislation in EC countries and possible conflicts with the Treaty of Rome.

27 See for instance Gary Becker 'A Theory of the Allocation of Time', *Economic Journal*, September 1965.

28 J.A. Kay, et al., *The Regulation of Retail Trading Hours*, London, Institute for Fiscal Studies, 1984, p.36.

29 S.M. Jaffer and C.N. Morris, *Sunday Trading and Employment*, Institute for Fiscal Studies, London 1985.

30 Submission by USDAW Scottish Division to the Confederation of Scottish Local Authorities, June 1990.

31 Frances Cairncross, 'Shopping Hours: The Options for Reform', Shopping Hours Reform Council, June 1992.

32 T. Burke and J.R. Shackleton, *Sunday, Sunday: The Issues in Sunday Trading*, London, Adam Smith Institute, 1989.

33 Ruth Lister, *Women's economic dependency and social security*, Manchester, Equal Opportunities Commission, Research Discussion Series 2, 1992.

34 See Lynda Bransbury, *Escaping From Dependency*, London, Rivers Oram Press/IPPR, forthcoming.

35 Hakim, 'Workforce Restructuring', op.cit.

36 Ibid.

37 Lister, *Women's economic dependency*, op.cit., pp.43–5.

38 Bransbury, *Escaping from Dependency*, op.cit.

39 Lister, *Women's Economic Dependency*, op.cit., p.71.

40 Bransbury, *Escaping from Dependency*, op.cit.; Lister, *Women's Economic Dependency*, op.cit.

41 *Price v Civil Service Commission and Another*, EA1/77.

42 Schuller and Walker, *The Time of Our Life*, op.cit., on which I have drawn for the whole of this section.
43 *Social Trends* 1990, Table 7.2.

7 The Challenge to Managers

1 'Managers "work too many hours" ', *Independent*, 20 January 1992.
2 Harriet Harman MP, *Time Gentlemen, Please*, December 1990.
3 A. Spurling, *Report of the Women in Higher Education Research Project*, Cambridge, Kings College, May 1990, pp.9–11.
4 Madeline Bunting, 'The cutting edge', *Guardian*, 9 April 1991.
5 Anne Montague, 'Doctors who are in double pain', *Guardian*, 18 September 1990.
6 TSB Equal Opportunities Programme, Briefing Papers and Press Release, 8 May 1991.
7 Opportunity 2000, *Summary of Goals and Action Plans of the Opportunity 2000 Campaign Organisations*, October 1991.
8 Institute of Manpower Studies, *Flexible manning: the way ahead*, IMS/Manpower Ltd, 1984.
9 'Dawn of a New Deal', *Personnel*, 22 October 1991.
10 Curson, *Flexible Patterns*, op.cit., p.183.
11 See for instance *Work and the Family: Carer-friendly employment practices*, London, IPM, 1990.
12 I am indebted to Bryn Davies of Union Pension Services for this calculation.
13 *Working Hours' Reforms*, op.cit.
14 Marsh, *Hours of Work*, op.cit., p.82.

8 The Challenge to Trade Unions

1 P. Rathkey, 'Trade unions, collective bargaining and reduced working time: a critical assessment', *Employee Relations*, 8, 1, 1986, pp.4–9.
2 Letter from Head of Management, Employment Policy Branch, British Coal to author, August 1991.
3 'New Proposed Working Practices in the British Deep Coal Mining Industry', Paper presented to NUM Conference, 1987.
4 TGWU, *Putting Children in the Picture: A TGWU Negotiator's Guide*, p.17.
5 U. Huws, J. Hurstfield, R. Holtmaat, *What Price Flexibility: The Casualisation of Women's Employment*, London, Low Pay Unit, 1989, p.35.
6 *Part-time work: NALGO Negotiating Guidelines*.
7 BIFU Research, *Term Time and V Time Working*, October 1990.
8 Huws, et al., *What Price Flexibility?*, op.cit., p.39.
9 Council of Civil Service Unions, statement on *Alternative Working Patterns*, 28 March 1989.
10 Karlsen, *Arbeidstid*, op.cit., p.22.

11 Seifert, '*Sozialvertragliche Arbeitszeitgestalung*', op.cit., concludes: 'the "normal working day" has by no means outlived its usefulness in guiding the formation of policies and regulations. Its role is, though, not quite that of a model for working hours policies. It assumes, instead, especially as the structuring of working hours becomes more diverse, the function of a normative standard for the evaluation of divergent types of working hours.'
12 Huws, et al., *What Price Flexibility?*, op.cit., p.41.

Conclusion

1 Fritz W. Scharpf, *Crisis and Choice in European Social Democracy*, New York, Cornell University Press, 1991.
2 Michael E. Porter, *The Competitive Advantage of Nations*, Basingstoke, Macmillan, 1990.
3 Hilary Metcalf and Patricia Leighton estimated that in 1987 1.1 million non-working women had 'O' levels or equivalent and a further 1 million had 'A' levels or higher. *The Under-Utilisation of Women in the Labour Market*, Institute of Manpower, 1989.
4 See Gosta Esping-Andersen, *The Three Worlds of Welfare Capitalism*, Oxford, Polity Press, 1990, for a pioneering analysis of the relationships between labour markets, welfare and women's employment.
5 R. Simpson, 'The Cost of Childcare Services' in *Childcare and Equal Opportunities*, Manchester, Equal Opportunities Commission, 1986.
6 Bronwen Cohen, *Child Care in a Modern Welfare System*, IPPR, 1991.